TRANSPLANTING FAITH

Portrait of a Miracle

Charles Gary Godwin

Charles Gary Godwin

XULON PRESS

Katie —

NOVEMBER 2013

Showing mercy to others
helps bring peace to your heart!

LUKE 6:36

Gary

DEDICATION

THORA SPITZFADEN GODWIN
February 14, 1918 – July 6, 2012

"IF THE SPIRIT OF HIM WHO RAISED JESUS FROM THE DEAD

DWELLS IN YOU,

HE WHO RAISED CHRIST JESUS FROM THE DEAD WILL

ALSO GIVE LIFE TO YOUR

MORTAL BODIES THROUGH HIS SPIRIT WHO DWELLS IN YOU."

Romans 8:11

Thanks to the mother of Wayne, Gary and Susan

TRANSPLANTING FAITH

CONTENTS

PREVIEW

*P*ulmonary disfunction taking a friend who gasps final breaths before my eyes. Sense the heart not pumping. Two lungs failing to function. Kidneys shut down. Intensive Care Unit room is tomb-like in quiet conversation. Visitor eyes glued to the ventilator, silenced in the off position. Rhythmic sight and sound ceasing. Thuuup, pssss, thuuup, pssss, thuuup, psssssssssssssssss. Silence. Death. Expressions of goodbye too late to be heard. You never forget the sight of death. Too many illnesses. Too much disease. Too few answers. Two deadly killers acting as grim reaper relatives.

Idiopathic Pulmonary Fibrosis (IPF) claims 40,000 deaths per year, equal to its better known cousin breast cancer. 40,000 deaths per year. One disease constantly spreading into the nation's consciousness. IPF, hardly a household name, claiming nearly as many victims in the United States as the better known killer. A deadly duo knit together by comparable annual death tolls. Regrettably, neither currently offers a solid solution or cure. Survival prospects do exist. Chemotherapy, surgery, and/or radiation treatment can add years to a cancer infested body. IPF demise, often slowed through a modest use of doctor prescribed steroids, carries its greatest enhanced life opportunity through lung transplant. Generously, one person's donor legacy leads to a lung recipient's gratitude. An IPF sufferer, I live in humble tribute to an unknown donor whose left lung helps sustain this 69 year old body.

Temporary relocation to Birmingham, Alabama, readied our lives for transplant. Breathing freely, wife Susan and I meander at an unhurried pace through the hills of Birmingham. Downtown, block after block, we view massive facilities known as the University of Alabama at Birmingham (UAB) medical complex. Maintaining modest exercise attached to an oxygen tank, one healthy pastime involved frequent walks along the paved, occasional tree-root-disrupted trail in Homewood. Kudos to city leaders for providing runners, walkers, and bike riders an exercise trail for lovers of the outdoors.

Returning to our Birmingham apartment home, my pulse rate quickens and anticipation level rises, hoping the incoming phone call would be UAB with "the call" to come to the hospital for transplant. Elevated expectations partially caused by knowledge that UAB, family, and close personal friends allegedly the only ones privy to that phone number. Mispronunciation of, and an extra "o" in the last name (Mr. Goodwin), a dead giveaway. Telemarketers obtaining supposed "do-not-call" secret information. Facing a life threatening disease, the intrusion seemed most egregious. "I don't care what you're selling, I'm awaiting a phone call leading to lung transplant. Goodbye." Or words to that effect. Six, count them, six calls from UAB for possible transplant. First five heightened anticipation. Each empty visit to UAB, however, producing a sinking feeling comparable emotionally to losing a T-Ball championship game. Having experienced both I can affirm that age and health issues do alter priorities.

Barriers arose frequently. Laugh or cry (we did) at moments of humor or sadness. From my viewpoint, trace the transplant experience, start to finish, beginning to end, alpha to omega. Raw emotions unveil moments of anger and frustration, doubts, and reassurance. Compassionate transplant team members quietly accommodating whether working in the surgical suite, recovery room or HTICU (Heart Thoracic Intensive Care Unit). Huge smiles about as prevalent as sun lamps in the surgical suite, seemingly kept at temperatures just a few degrees north of freezing. These folks mean business, and my life is their business.

With a "where the heck am I?" eye-opening recovery the day after transplant, I must trust family recollection of my incessant chatter. My memory bank misplaced that deposit. Nothing. Zip. Nada. Zero recollection. One day lost. Do I hear Twilight Zone music?

Transplant accomplished, share an "uh-oh" minute dedicated to my cardiologist. Speaking of dedication, I often wrapped myself in the comforting arms of loving caregiver Susan and supportive family and friends. Struggling to add years to my life, couple that comforting sensation with a search for God's desire for those extra years. Cheer a "new birthday" gift from an unknown donor. Ominous gray coloration of the diseased left lung replaced by a glorious, sunset pink hue of an organ surgeon described as a "beautiful lung."

OK, so my beauty resides inside. Outside, the snake-like scar shows no sign of the fifty-seven staples closing the surgeon's scalpel path. With an erasable marker trace the incision. Start a line slightly under and to the southeast of your left breast. Closely guide the marker in a swirling pattern near the scapula, slithering spineward. Professional surgical hands work swiftly and efficiently. Open gently, extract diseased lung and replace with that "beautiful lung." Merge the two skin flaps, close the incision, and move the patient to recovery. Two hours and forty-five minutes, start to finish. A round of golf takes longer. Heck, my driving range and putting green preparation for golf takes more time.

Whatever your life story, I pray that God touches you in some affirming way during your lifetime as He touched Susan and me during this remarkably miraculous journey. May hope never leave your heart. Now, in honor of Brian and Mickey and the other Charles Gary, the rest of the story.

<u>To My Unknown Donor</u>

Dear friend, on September 28, 2010, you and I became one through the transition of transplant as you loosed the binding chains of earthly existence. Life ebbed from your mortal form. Saddened, moist eyes and tear-stained faces probably fixed on your life departure. Some images last a lifetime.

I wonder what memories remain from your final hours. From your life. I wonder if cessation of suffering brought gladness through the sadness. I wonder if family/friends/ loved ones know you donated life for two strangers. My transplant sibling added life with the heart of the donor whose left lung resides in me. I am humbly grateful to be part of the family.

Know that two of your organ recipients share a calling. Organ donation and faith in transplant surgery are life-saving stories to be told. I am forever indebted to you whose donation shares life with me. Thank you. God bless you.

Gary's Palm Cross

Charles Gary Godwin
Left Lung Transplant
UAB
9.28.10

CHAPTER 1

DOGS, ELEPHANTS, BIG GREEN TORPEDO

"Come to me, all who labor and are
heavy laden, and I will give you rest"
Matthew 11:28

Thunderstorms. Power outage. Air conditioner? Not cooling. Refrigerator? Food warming. Hot Water? Turned to cold. Television? Not available. Icing on the cake? OMG! Highlighting the unthinkable for an oxygen dependent IPF sufferer? No electricity powered concentrator. Uh-oh! Oxygen alert. Oxygen alert. Somebody help this breathing impaired patient. Blessed angels Parker and Phyllis invited us to spend time in the "Godwin Suite" portion of their Vestavia Hills home. Their guest bedroom renamed due to frequent use during our University of Alabama at Birmingham (UAB) visits in preparation for transplant listing. Grabbing four to-go meals from one of the Birmingham area's 4000+ eateries, nighttime lighting guided our path to the land of electricity. Leisurely mealtime conversation stilled when local television meteorologists informed that thunderstorms had rumbled north and east. Promising to revisit if electricity awaited restoration to our apartment, Susan and I returned to the land of darkness.

Whoops. No outside lights. Major indicator electricity was missing. Recalling the invitation, Susan and I flashlighted our way to pack necessities for transport to the Godwin Suite. The 40-pound concentrator remained for placement in our vehicle's trunk. As Susan's path from the parking lot to the apartment was lighted one step at a time by flashlight, she counted once more on God's grace and mercy. "Lord, thank you for electricity and please restore it soon." Walking into the living room, holding the flashlight on the concentrator as I wrapped its cord for transit, God responded. Lights? On. AC? Cooling. Refrigerator? Chilling. Water? Hot. TV? Available. Thanks Lord.

Combined, oxygen and nitrogen comprise about 99% of the air we inhale. Eliminate availability and trouble follows. Can you say BREATHE? For those suffering with lung disorders/disease, oxygen necessity becomes paramount. Try climbing a flight of stairs without supplemental oxygen - breathless instantly. Mow the grass. Walk the dog. Shop for groceries. Serve, cook or bartend in a restaurant. Manage inventory and sales at a convenience store - on your feet all day. Ordinary life events present new challenges. Convince your mind to move your body. Good luck.

September 18, 2009. The oxygen odyssey begins, unaware of the frightening events to unfold within the next eight months. The small, portable tank ("dog" size) accompanied my travels of short duration (about 50 minutes) and my visits and workouts at the Thomas Hospital Wellness Center. Dispensed at a level of six liters per minute, treadmill time was regulated by movement of the tank register needle down to "you're about out of oxygen." Electricity at home made this a non-issue as my stationary concentrator pumped breath constantly and consistently into my IPF lungs. Blessings! Appreciative of expansive supply, I choose to live remaining days not tethered to an oxygen tank. Praying for a healthy lung, thanking God, that's how life will happen. My Fairhope oxygen supplier (thanks Denise) graciously provided emergency canisters of oxygen for our relocation trip to Birmingham. Hopefully we would not need the supply. Thankfully, we had it. Size didn't matter: the small container (known as a "dog"), the medium size cylinder (called an "elephant") and the lovely, almost taller-than-me big green torpedo (known with affection as "the big green torpedo"). Shape defines the nomenclature for the final size listed.

Movement to our temporary home should have included at least an initial supply of oxygen to replace the 02 tanks left behind. Oops! Nothing at our apartment. Quick, slightly panicked call to Tonja, another of our UAB "angel nurses." "Let me make a few phone calls," she advised. Short story: her "few phone calls" turned into oxygen tanks for me, her south Alabama buddy. Tonja's life-saving calls seemingly connected straight to God. Daily wakeup offers proof that our oxygen supply sustained us through another restful night, granting survival for one more day. Peaceful rest comes from faith and belief that our lungs will function properly. Faith, without question.

Tuesday, October 12, 2010 6:21 PM, CDT One regulator. Check. One hand cart. Check. One stationary concentrator. Check. Fifteen, yep fifteen, unused oxygen cannisters ("elephant" size) carted away by Chris to another in need. Plus, don't forget the big green torpedo, slightly used but not abused. Yesterday those fifteen lined my apartment foyer and the "torpedo" found safety tucked inside the guest bedroom closet. Today? Joyfully returned during another "rite of passage" day. Prayers of thanks for those in the oxygen supply business. Thanks, too, for son Matthew in town to help with my care. Yet one more incredible blessing from a gracious God.

Reflection: Children. Unfiltered language. Stage whispers. Regular trips to Target for groceries always included seeing children in some form of adult company during this afternoon adventure. An oxygen tank protruding from the grocery cart, the cannula plugging my nostrils, I became an easy target for childlike stage whisper questions and stares.

"Mommy, is that man sick?" "Gran, what's that man have in his nose?" "Daddy, what's that tank thing in his cart?" Natural questions from inquisitive young minds. Switch places. Fairhope's Thomas Hospital Wellness Center. Alicia, Betsy, Edwina and Amy coordinating exercise regimens keeping diseased lungs healthy as possible. The part-time pastor spies the treadmilling stranger sucking air from a portable oxygen supply. "Excuse me. You obviously have some lung issue. Do you mind if I pray for you?" Do I mind? Pray on pastor. Review these two scenarios. One a little bit embarrassing. "How can I avoid those stares? I don't like this." The other? Humbly grateful for a prayer-giving stranger. Can't hide the oxygen tanks. Living in fear of what others think or say, I faced a very sheltered life; no shopping, no church, no movies, no eating out, no life, hermit-like existence. Does some private fear hold you captive? Are you embarrassed to be seen in public with your own oxygen-canister-type story? Do you fear child-like questions? Which life do you choose? Without oxygen, I'm not here. Goodbye embarrassment.

Phyllis and Parker

Chapter 2

Living With Ughs

"With man it is impossible, but not with God. For all things are possible with God." Mark 10:27

Ferocious. Ugly. Insidious. Deadly. Multiple descriptions fit IPF. Scarring of the lungs chokes life-sustaining oxygen. Shortness of breath, for even menial tasks, an early IPF indicator. CT scans, x-rays and pulmonary function tests help identify the killer. New cases increase by nearly 50,000 each year, and the Pulmonary Fibrosis Foundation in Chicago claims that number might be higher. Approximately 150,000 to 200,000 Americans (about one-third the population of Wyoming) live with IPF. Death relentlessly claims roughly 40,000 victims per year. Recent statistics place the number of annual lung transplants slightly south of 2,000. Slumped shoulders sadly reflect IPF sufferers facing odds of lung transplantation at 1-in-100. Pretty poor odds. Transfer the IPF lung transplant rate to the 100-member United States Senate. One in 100 would be granted immunity. Scary? Ask your United States Senator.

Lung tissue scarring by IPF restricts oxygen flow to the body. Following initial diagnosis, IPF serves as a 3 – 5 year sentence on death row. Age, gender, height, weight have little bearing on IPF survival; the disease is an equal opportunity killer. With no defined cause for the fibrosis, there is no known cure. Read that last line one more time. Absorb it slowly. Repeat in your mind "... there is no known cure." Sobering news heard by the patient. Facing a diminished lifetime and an accelerating downhill slide, Susan and I opted to fight for my life. Balancing highs and lows, stretching the limits of faith, we embarked on an unknown and unexpected journey.

IPF rattles the spirit while scarring the lungs. Heard through a stethoscope, the sounds of breathing liken to the noise of stepping on cracked glass. C-r-r-u-u-n-n-c-h-h. C-r-r-u-n-n-c-h-h. And comforting words from the physician? Hear it again: "with no known cause, there is no known cure." Gee, why don't I feel better? Demoralized, IPF sufferers seek treatment centers like the University of Alabama at Birmingham. Treating IPF victims who live mainly in reasonable proximity to Birmingham, UAB offers a collection of spirit driven caregivers. UAB staffers provide a spiritual experience not unlike church worship. Kind, compassionate, caring. Just what you need and just like family. I've often asked if hospital personnel attend a special class devoted to touching a patient's spirit while working to correct physical deficiencies. Nope. Just a special selection process attuned to patient care.

September 18, 2009. Life in Fairhope changed, with delivery of my initial supply of oxygen; a large, stable concentrator and a smaller, transportable variety. Existence at home relied on a dual nostril, 50-foot long single line cannula. Life-sustaining oxygen flowing from a bulky concentrator to deteriorating lungs. My ego detested each moment I had to suck artificial air. Ugh. Ugh. Ugh. "Hey buddy, where would you be without that artificial air?" H-m-m-m-m. So much for the Ughs!

Accepting a diagnosis incompatible with my generally good health proved difficult. Doctor assessments, supported by myriad pulmonary function tests, verified presence of the IPF villain. Oh no. "Upon further review, the ruling stands ..." Terminology passes from the football field to medical examination rooms. Very comforting. Given a death sentence placed mortality squarely in the crosshairs of my IPF rifle sights. Crisis. Must be time for God.

I didn't know much about this fibrosis beast prior to learning of its life-shortening existence. Reaching Medicare age of sixty-five, diminishing energy indicated my trolley car was heading downhill faster than a San Francisco cable car with no brakes. Following an episode of breath shortness in the summer of 2006, I landed in the emergency room and an overnight bed at Thomas Hospital in Fairhope. Multiple tests showed early signs of possible IPF attacking an otherwise healthy body. Medication, diet, and exercise blended to control my Type II diabetes, diagnosed years earlier. Forty years of a cigarette smoking habit had been extinguished April 2, 2001. On advice from a local pulmonologist I began the ritual of a six month checkup. Sounding like music to my lungs, the first checkup offered a year's reprieve from more testing. Sensation likened to killing the queen in a giant red ant hill. Hooray! Small victories count mightily for those suffering life-altering diseases. The fibrosis had not diminished nor had there been any advancing invasion of the lungs. Sounds OK to me. Modest episodes of breath shortness failed to prevent most normal activities but just as 9/11/01 changed the landscape of New York City, so a visit there in September 2009 added a new chapter to this story. Susan and I desired to see it all and do it all. We wanted a big bite from the Big Apple. Sadly for us, the apple bit back!

 *Reflection:* Curves, turns and changes of direction frequently weave their way into our lives. Birth. Baptism. Kindergarten. Teen years. College. Marriage. Children. Employment. Retirement. Illness. Death. Each segment of our journey offers challenges and opportunities. My parents and grandparents suffered the Great Depression. Perhaps Ben Franklin's "penny saved is a penny earned" statement carried relevance to those inflicted with the horrific aspects of too-little money and too-much need. With lives crumbling around them, parents and grandparents questioned their

religion. "God, where are you? Why do you allow this to happen?" Pleading cries drifted heavenward. Recollections of God's people and their forty years in the desert visit the mind. Regardless of circumstances, we expect the best. Diseases should be non-existent or treatable. An answer should accompany every problem. When life sails smoothly forward we tell God we're OK, can handle situations ourselves. Life altering circumstances remind of our reliance on the Father. He never leaves us. Constantly remind yourself of those few words during times of gratitude and times of travail. You don't need a transplant to live a life centered in Him. At what time do you think God left your side? Why do you feel that way? Where is He now? What are you thankful for today? Have you opened a lemonade stand with life's lemons? God's possibilities are endless. If we didn't have the bad, how would we ever know the good? Sometimes hard and sometimes easy; in all circumstances give thanks.

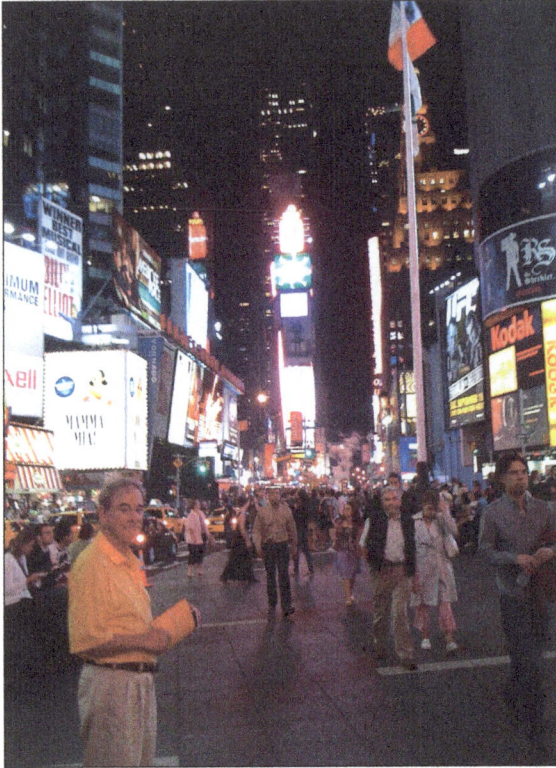

Times Square New York City

CHAPTER 3

FOLLOW DAISY'S LEAD

❦

". . . for I have learned in whatever situation
I am to be content."
Philippians 4:11

September 9, 2009. The Big Apple. New York City. Some business. Some pleasure. A September 11th birthday girl, Susan definitely felt the adventurous spirit of this special trip. Eye straining sights, taxi horn and ambulance siren dominated sounds saturated the senses. Empire State Building, Times Square, new Yankee Stadium — the Yankees lost that day — Broadway production of "Phantom of the Opera," tourist watercraft motoring around Manhattan Island and past the Statue of Liberty. Hudson River spray kisses exposed cheeks. Impressive. Concurrently, my lungs seared like a raw ribeye sizzling on a grill. I attributed lack of breath to multiple walking forays inhaling the vehicle-generated stale air of NYC.

Reality greeted my return to our southern Alabama home. Unfiltered breathing issues permeated diseased lungs. The scheduled annual pulmonologist visit advanced by thirty days. New x-rays confirmed a worsening fibrosis. The singular treatment alternative offered by the doctor was steroids (no thanks). Seeking other choices, Susan and I initiated a desperate search (Internet to start) for information about this debilitating disease. The news? Not encouraging. IPF defines no specific cause and offers no specific cure. Sometimes the lung scarring zooms forward like a race car speeding to the checkered flag. Sometimes it ambles at its own pace and other times it creeps forward as if desiring a second place finish in its race with a tortoise. The disease definitely defines itself.

Our IPF research pointed to Dr. Victor J. Thannickal, UAB director of the division of Pulmonary, Critical Care and Sleep Disorders. Transplanted to Birmingham from the University of Michigan, Dr. Thannickal and a bulging briefcase carried copious notes about extensive research work with the NOX4 enzyme. Maybe, just maybe, there exists a glimmer of hope for IPF sufferers. No miraculous breakthrough yet for IPF, but the research shows promising signs of slowing or stopping the disease spread.

Also punching a ticket south from Michigan, scientist and newly titled PhD, Louise Hecker. A tenacious researcher, Dr. Hecker partners with Dr. Thannickal to find answers for diseases like IPF. Seeking grants for additional clinical research also occupies working hours. Dr. Hecker, not far removed from receipt of her Doctor of Philosophy, serves UAB as a research scientist. Her introduction to us came during an infusion session as part of my participation in a clinical trial attempting to solve the IPF puzzle. Forget the stereotypical researcher; her nose is not forever embedded between the dual eyepieces of a microscope. Meeting new people, Louise quickly shares the warmth of her Italian heritage and the grace of newfound southern gentility. Don't forget her million-dollar smile and direct, eye-to-eye contact in conversation. This youthful dynamo's research will produce positive results due to tenacity in finding a solution for the IPF affecting me - her poster child.

October 13, 2009. An unexpected bonus surfaces from our initial visit to UAB. My attending physician stepping through the exam room door? Dr. Victor Thannickal himself. As the division director, he manages time to see patients and perform multiple administrative affairs that come with responsibilities of his position. He proved to be one of God's special "angels" sent to guide Susan and me through this ordeal.

Recognizing the severity of my illnesses (including diabetes), he offered the opportunity to participate in a clinical trial for a drug that holds some hope for IPF treatment. No promises, of course. As a matter of fact, I could be the 1-in-4 trial participants whose monthly infusion therapy is placebo based. But hey, what's to lose? If this trial doesn't help me, it may provide answers for future IPF sufferers. "For as much as you have done unto the least of these . . ." Agreeing to the clinical trial, I was concurrently placed in a preliminary pulmonary review.

In February 2010 I labored through a week-long battery of tests to determine my viability as a potential candidate for transplant surgery. Body-invading testing, excruciating at times, would lead to one of three eventualities: (1) my overall health was satisfactory enough for immediate placement on the transplant waiting list; (2) I was still a candidate for "listing," but some health issues needed attention before my name occupied space on the waiting list; (3) medical management combining diet, exercise and medication offered a reasonable course of action. Susan and I prayed for door #1; the answer offered by transplant team member Dr. Keith Wille was door #2. Arterial blockage sounded alarm bells for the vascular surgeon whose determination was crucial to my next course of treatment. Setback it seemed, but minor compared to a normally undisturbed, rock solid faith. My ongoing mantra? "Let's go. I'll do whatever it takes."

Awaiting our next medical option, I continued an exercise regimen that included a 36-visit program for pulmonary rehab at a treatment facility in Foley, Alabama, fifteen miles south of our Fairhope home. Seeking a stronger body, I also engaged in three to four times per week visits to the Thomas Hospital Wellness Center. Why exercise when I've been told no transplant? Simple. With a strengthening faith, I believed I could reverse UAB's "no" to a "yes." Interestingly, Dr. Wille, the physician who gave me the "no" is now burdened as my primary care coordinator. Blessed with Dr. Thannickal's initial care, Dr. Wille's mission with this patient includes follow-ups for: 1) my lung transplant (post-surgery), (2) my diabetes,

(3) a back fracture suffered four weeks before transplantation, (4) 4-stent insertion to remove arterial blockage, (5) a heart attack and two-stent insertion two days after lung transplant and (6) a dental difficulty that resulted in extraction of remnants of a destroyed three-tooth bridge. Burden? You betcha. Faith on call? Constantly. Holy cow, does your endurance level reside at an all time high?

Reflection: Awaiting a lung transplant or a heart transplant (I do have a transplant sibling), stay the course. Suffering any medical difficulty or facing liver, lung, kidney, heart, or any other transplant, keep your commitment dedicated to an improved life. Seek prayerful support. Do not quit. Never ever give up. One of my new friends, seeking admission to the transplant list, said of one UAB mandatory test that requires a passing grade: "I can't do the six-minute walk. They won't let me walk two minutes, rest two minutes, walk two, rest two and walk the final two." I told her the walk was easy; hard part was getting ready. "This is not a sprint but a six-minute marathon. Take your time, pace yourself and keep the faith that '. . . with God all things are possible.'" Stepping out with a renewed spirit of faithful dedication, Daisy pushed aside her physical and mental pain. She banished the obstacle of a self-imposed roadblock.

Allow Daisy's dedication and strength of spirit to inspire you. Keep the faith. Work hard. Remember what can be accomplished with God's help. Daisy now lives, works, and exercises in the spirit with a newly transplanted lung. Thanks be to God. What mental roadblock halts any of your physical accomplishments? What perceived obstacles deter your successful achievement? Which drives you more: can't do or *can do*? Excellent work though they do, the Alabama Organ Center (AOC) lacks the organ that transplants desire into your body or transplants faith into your heart. As Daisy reminds in her email signatures: "Let your attitude determine your altitude." How high are you flying?

Mz. Daisy
2012 Celebration of Life Picnic

CHAPTER 4

TRANSPLANT'S "TEN-STEPPER"

❧

". . .for it is the Lord your God who goes with you.
He will not leave you or forsake you."
Deuteronomy 31:6

OK, now what? I've got it; I desperately want to eliminate it. Remember time frames? This is the 3 – 5 year death sentence disease. Don't know how or why I got on death row, awaiting the finality of life, but thankfully this prison has a most compassionate warden. My friend Tammie offers comforting words: "Gary, God wants you well. He has more for you to do. Believe it!" With a spiritual connection worthy of consideration for sainthood, Tammie steers me away from the "pity-pat pitifuls" straight to the ". . . listen to what God has ahead for your life." Spiritual brothers and sisters come in all shapes, sizes, and genders. No "down-in-the-mouthers" during the trials of devastating illness. Give me laughter. Give me smiles. Give me hope! Pray with me and for me. Ask your friends to ask their friends to pray for you too. Ring God's telephone day and night. Thankfully, He never sleeps.

My recollection of the disease-confirming visit with the pulmonologist was somewhat numbing. "You've got a problem." "OK," I respond, "how do we treat it?" "Wish it was that easy, but it's not. You've got IPF, Idiopathic Pulmonary Fibrosis." "OK," I respond again; "how do we treat it?" "There is no known cure at this time." "So," I retort, "what do we do?" "Well, the disease carries a 3–5 year life expectancy from date of diagnosis." Over and over; 3–5 years, 3–5 years. My initial indicator occurred in June 2006, three years earlier. H-m-m-m-m-m. "Steroids may offer solace in retarding the spread of this lung-damaging disease but today there aren't many choices." Where, I wonder, is my personal scientist with required answers.

Give up, throw up or stand up and fight. IPF or other devastating disease, what's your choice? Hopefully, you choose life. Now you become a fighter. Here's what to expect in the days ahead and how to prepare yourself for the "fight of, and for, your life." Ten steps. Some common sense. Some hard. Some easier. All ten critical for IPF patients and some carrying importance for any debilitating illness. From personal experience, here's my Top Ten list for things to do for transplant preparation/recovery.

#1. PRAY! Especially pray for your donor and his/her loved ones. Someone made, or will make, a conscious decision to extend life for a stranger. The cost? Steep. Somebody reaches mortality. Knowledge of the donor, or how his/her organ(s) became available, is inconsequential. Pray in peace for an unknown stranger, and soak incredible calm in your mind, body, and spirit. Pray with loved ones or alone. Add links to that prayer chain. Pray with your pastor, minister, priest, or spiritual soul mate. Ring God's phone constantly. He always answers in His time and in His ways. He determines what is best for you. Pray for placement on the transplant waiting list. Pray for the surgery when that becomes imminent. Pray for the doctors and nurses who will perform and assist with your surgery. Pray for rapid healing and recovery. Pray for modest complications and the strength to overcome them. Pray from your heart with thanks to God.

#2. PREPARE! Twice weekly, I walk our garbage can the fifty or so steps down our driveway and to the street for next day collection. No preparation necessary for this pre-transplant five minute adventure. Preparation differs drastically for inclusion on the transplant wait list. Entering an unknown world you undergo extensive physical, mental, and emotional testing. No study guides or manuals. Instead, write down your questions, and someone during that testing period can provide answers. Prepare yourself physically. Smoking? Quit. Tough one but very possible because life is so precious. Overweight? Lose pounds. Couch potato? Get up and exercise, with your doctor's affirmation. Fifteen minutes daily is a good starting point. Breathing difficulties? Use your portable oxygen supply. I spent many treadmill hours at Thomas Hospital Wellness Center with my oxygen cord coiled like a snake around the treadmill's handlebars. You want extended life? This part is not easy. Just ask Daisy.

#3. SUPPORT SYSTEM! Family, friends, acquaintances, strangers. Support for surgery and recovery is critical care. UAB mandates caregiver contact information for your post-transplant period. Your body groans with new physical limitations. Maybe a wheelchair or walker assists your movement. When Susan and I moved to Birmingham, we had a limited circle of friends (4) outside our medical friends. Although Parker, Phyllis, Erica, and Brian provided extraordinary support, their lives precluded 24/7 availability. Susan's constant vigilance offered minimum personal respite. Come on family. Come on friends. Dear friends from church, including both our priests, visited on multiple occasions. Our first visitor was church friend Julie and daughter Corte, and our last visitors at the apartment were church friends David and Georgi. My brother Wayne and his wife Vera flew in to celebrate my birthday. Were she not caring for our 94 year old mother, my sister Sue would have visited from New Orleans. Other dear church friends came to give Susan relief on the weekends. Sweet Suzanne surprised with a visit on Susan's birthday. Fellow church friend Ceil visited on her journey to northeast Alabama and joined our anniversary dinner. Spiritual brother Mike and son Matthew made multiple visits. Support system? No question. Be ready. Tell them to expect your call.

#4. CLINICAL TRIALS AND TESTING! Based on your health circumstances (immediate transplant need or delayed time frame), you may participate in a clinical trial for a drug that might be the key which unlocks the IPF door. Accept the opportunity. Expenses are paid by the drug company supplying the clinical medicines. Even if your trial involves placebos (which you might be taking) you provide vital information to be used for future patients. If the trial is not working (my case) you could be removed and possibly changed to another trial. Potential transplant listing could be in the offing. Recommendations from a week's worth of testing will determine that eventuality. If the testing shows you to be ineligible for placement on the list (in my case arterial blockage), find out why. Ask how to change those circumstances (heart cath for me). Worth pursuing the ultimate gift of transplant, move quickly to change life aspects that need changing. I endured the heart cath, cleared the blockage with four stents and moved to the transplant waiting list four weeks later. Preparing for the unthinkable, determine for yourself that the reward is worth the risk. Thankfully, I did.

#5. ECONOMICS. Transplantation is not an inexpensive procedure. Expected cost for my surgery and post surgical care was three hundred to four hundred thousand dollars. Not exactly "walking around pocket change." Medicare and Tricare for Life provided exceptional coverage and significantly reduced my bill. Many insurance companies cover the bulk of the expenses but you may still owe hundreds or thousands of dollars. A hospital staff social worker, acting as your compass, can guide a path to sources which assist with expenses. Don't be afraid to ask about covered charges. Check with your company's insurance representative, or the company human resources department. Consider the possibility of relocation and the expense involved.

Locate as close as possible to your transplant center of choice. For some friends who live close to UAB that facility was a natural choice. My friend Larry from southern Mississippi chose Ochsner Hospital in New Orleans. Hospital facility closeness (two hours away) is critical for the delicate lung. With multiple transplant facilities in the country, the search for a nearby facility should be short. Knowing we were 259 miles south, a two hour trip would have involved NASCAR type speeds. Not really our best option.

UAB's Townhouse offered one alternative but a corporate, turnkey apartment became our six month residence. Social workers can provide lists of nearby living facilities for whichever transplant center you choose. For assistance with noncovered expenses, some patients and their family/friends choose to hold fund raisers of various types. Consider asking a family member or friend to accept this responsibility. Bottom line? If you need a transplanted lung (organ) to extend your life, be proactive.

#6. COMMUNICATION. Showing my age, remember the joke about the three forms of communication: tell-a-phone, tell-a-graph (really old!) and tell-a-woman? More updated communication forms include cell phone, texting, Facebook, twitter, and by the time you get this book, probably another dozen on the horizon. Serious illness is no laughing matter, though, and family, friends and loved ones enjoy updates about a patient's progress. Multiple phone calls wear on the loved one making those calls. Though impersonal, electronic communication gives a break, physically and emotionally, to the caregiver. Prepare a list of those you want to keep informed of progress through the transplant process. Cell numbers and email addresses are most important. CaringBridge became our primary communications vehicle. It's a free website, devoted to making the communications process less demanding on the caregiver. You record changing events, and there's an opportunity for responses. Though personal contact is still important for loved ones, updated electronic progress reports reach a broader audience at one time. I promise you, the responses are heartwarming and extremely supportive. Reminds me of an "electronic hug," available when needed.

#7. EXERCISE. Declined for transplant listing due to heart blockage issues, my initial reaction was "what?" Recovery from the shock turned quickly to proactivity. "OK," I told the docs. "Since that won't work, what's the best plan B?" Turns out I had already been working on plan B - exercise. Thirty-six visits to the pulmonary rehab program at a Foley (AL) hospital strengthened portions of my lung not yet damaged. Wendy was the first of three fitness friends with whom I shared a love-hate relationship. I loved them for what they made me do (exercises), and I hated them for what they made me do (exercises). Facing folks like me on a regular basis, they all have infectious smiles that alleviate the discomfort of exercise. My transplant doctors gave all of them credit for placing me in a fairly healthy position for medical care both before and after surgery. The healing process shortens your hospital stay. Fight, fight, fight the strong desire to give up on this aspect of the transplant process. Coordinate this regimen with your physicians. Blessed with a healthy lung, I still exercise 3 - 5 days a week. Thanks Lord.

#8. DIMINISH DISAPPOINTMENT. IPF patients live ticking time-bomb lives daily. Statistically, realization acknowledges the 3 - 5 year life span from date of first diagnosis. Today, organ transplant remains the best option available for IPF sufferers. Sadly, not everyone qualifies immediately and some may not qualify at all. Some, like me, will be considered once health issues are resolved (remember my clogged arteries?). Disappointments abound in the process. "You're overweight," "you're too old," "you have arterial blockage," "your other health issues disqualify you," "you need more exercise," "you need to quit smoking," blah, blah, blah. Expect disappointment. Expect to overcome disappointment. Your hospital's medical staff is experienced in helping patients plow through times of disappointment, offering encouragement and hope. Recognize disappointing days lie ahead (my transplant came on visit #6). Do not be overwhelmed. Do not be discouraged. Believe that your donor organ is coming soon. At the height of disappointment, refer back to #1.

#9. ENCOURAGEMENT. Abundance of encouraging words, thoughts, and actions flow freely from the hospital staff. Expect to be up and moving the day after surgery. "Say what?" Get ready because it's coming. You receive more than enough coddling from family and staff so concentrate on movement as soon as possible post surgery. Someone will walk with you and encourage you to take as large a step as you can, and repeat the process often. Returning to our apartment after treatment at UAB for a fractured back, physical therapist Tina thrilled this patient, waiting to show exercises designed for my specific injury. Her tender nudging to expand my training regimen was softened by that infectious smile and compassionate attitude. Tina encourages, always nearby when I was doing exercises and always gently pushing me to do a "little bit more," but with that sweet smile. Be proactive in your recovery. Don't focus of what you can't do, but on what you can do.

Remembering our childhood, crawling came before walking, which came before running. All three were learned responses. Be patient with yourself. Encourage visits from encouraging people. Banish nay-sayers and pessimists. Work with an "encourager companion." When you get better, become an encourager yourself. Helping another IPF sufferer helps you more.

#10. HONOR YOUR DONOR! Transplant injects new life into your body. Lung, heart, liver, kidney, whatever the organ you now merge with part of another person. Chances are you may never know the donor or circumstances that led to death. What matters? You enjoy new life. When you decide to not buckle that seatbelt, think of your donor. When exercise becomes a dreaded burden, think of your donor. When the nicotine desire filters deeply in your lungs, think of your donor. When that banana split obsession, with the cherry on top, tickles the taste buds two-three times per week, think of your donor. Deciding "couch potato" status with your new organ is satisfactory for your added years, think of your donor. Driving after one-too-many adult beverages? Think of your donor. Zooming 85 miles per hour, passing all on the interstate, think of your donor. You have added life because someone left this life. Honor your donor!

Reflection: Unknowing. Untested. Fear. Life's new and different experiences can color our imaginations with no substance necessary. Unlike children, to whom life is one big new experience, we draw on past life events and resulting consequences to temper future thoughts and actions. For most, transplant is a new, one-time experience. Statistics present hard facts which help determine our reaction to transplant. Missing from that equation is our emotional factor. How does transplant work? Will I feel different with another's body part in my body? Will I be emotionally changed and subject to mood swings? How long do I take medications? How many medicines do I take? Will I feel different based on my donor's history? Are complications part of the deal? Answers for many questions come from our physicians. Pre-owned organ means new life. Just as in life, however, a used organ comes with no warranty. No 10 years or 100,000 miles. Best way to overcome the fear factor? Refer to #1. You have a tremendous resource with your soul mate and prayer partner. Share life with that individual. Happiness follows your choice.

Brother Wayne and son Matthew in town
helping with home repairs and grounds maintenance
prior to Birmingham relocation

Chapter 5

Strap On Boots and Let's Ride

*"For the eyes of the Lord range throughout the
earth to strengthen those whose hearts are
fully committed to him."*
2 Chronicles 16:9

3:55am, Saturday, May 29, 2010. Disturbing an otherwise peaceful sleep, the ringing phone announces another life changing event. The news permanently a safe deposit item stored in my memory bank. The first phone call: "Mr. Godwin, this is UAB transplant. We may have a lung for you." The University of Alabama at Birmingham (UAB) phone voice sounded calm and reassuring. My public speaking trained voice, however, quivered with anticipation. Gently, but with a degree of urgency, I helped awaken wife Susan, cuddled comfortably on "her side" of the bed. Is this my time already? If UAB had a residency requirement of seven days in order to qualify for a lung transplant this day would not have happened; our arrival in Birmingham coming one day shy of a week earlier. Recognizing the same frequent message given over the next six months, my time is not always God's time. Guess whose time counts more?

"Was it only six days earlier that we checked into turnkey corporate housing? Our new temporary residence is for how long?" "As long as it takes," spoke the inner voice. 1275 square feet of two-bedroom, two bath apartment living. Two-hundred-fifty-nine miles north of our permanent residence in Fairhope, Alabama. Only three miles measure our travel distance to Mobile Bay and the beloved Fairhope pier. Three mountain ranges in Birmingham with expansive views offer an incredible elevation differential for a couple from southern Alabama. Birmingham's mountaintops or Fairhope's seashore, both provide glances of the beauty inherent in God's creation.

Normal life does not begin at 3:55 am for us in either our Birmingham or Fairhope location. But IPF changes normal life. Any family struck by this disease, or any serious illness, can attest to lives being permanently changed. Most importantly, your faith faces severe testing. Listen to the words probably heard frequently by God. "OK Lord, why me?" "I don't smoke, Lord; never have." "I smoked for forty years, Lord, but gave it up ten years ago." "I live in an environment free of factory smoke and smog." "Lord, I eat healthy and go to church every Sunday." "God, why are you picking on me? I don't deserve this." "I've got a wife and three children, Lord, and what will they do without me?" Questions. Questions. Questions.

Time to ring up a little faith, best described in Hebrews 11:1 as ". . . the assurance of things hoped for but not yet seen." Easy? Not on your life. So simple to be appreciative of God when life is full of sunshine and roses, when He answers prayers to satisfy our purposes. But God never moves and always loves His children and answers prayers. Sometimes, we don't understand or appreciate the response. Could He have a better answer at a later moment? Video on the ten o'clock news.

Earlier thoughts race through my mind as Susan efficiently maneuvers us to UAB. Privately quiet, I sense Susan's elevated excitement level somewhat equal to that of her front seat passenger. Without driving responsibilities my mind turns to recollection of the somewhat numbing, disease-confirming visit with the pulmonologist. "You've got a problem called IPF. There is no known cure at this time. The disease carries a 3 – 5 year life expectancy from date of diagnosis. Steroids have proven to be of some help but as of today, there aren't many choices." Organ transplant, huh? Well, let's strap on the boots and saddle the horses; it's time to ride!

Our Birmingham journey deducted one-hundred-eighty-eight (188) days from our lives. More importantly, actions during that period added new life to a diseased body. And 5.29.10, the first phone call. The first indication that a healthy lung, sized to fit my body, was available. Sized to fit evokes images of the 16x32 long sleeve shirt coupled with new slacks either too tight or too loose, depending on current circumstances. Think of an emotion; I probably experienced it. Checking in during other than normal business hours can be tricky, but thanks for security. Into the elevator, press "5" and move into a new realm. Heart pounding, footsteps quickening, my pre-5:00 am arrival is greeted by empty hallways. Singular noise coming from footsteps moving right-left, right-left, in rhythm, along surgically clean floors. One lonely figure, the on-duty charge nurse, welcomes me. Susan joins after parking the car. We learn the routine. "If you want to save your oxygen hook into ours" offers the nurse. Kindly considerate. Thanks.

While I relished the attention, my heart rate rapidly elevated. "OK, Mr. Godwin. We need some blood samples." Aha. My first indication that UAB surely had a special holding place for the "Godwin Blood Bank." So much blood matching is required for transplant patients. The questionnaire needs to be completed. Extensive. Signatures remind of signing the mountainous pile of papers for a home mortgage. "Are you a right lung, left lung or both?" asks the charge nurse. "Good question, but just in case can I sign authorization for all of the above?" "No problem here. Oh, can we use some of your blood sample for experimental purposes?" Who would say no? Multiple machines, tubes and probes hooked up to measure heart rate, and oxygen saturation level, and blood pressure and the EKG machine. And the oxygen. And the IVs. Need to remember those extra needles in your arm when you head for the head (restroom). Lack of memory just one time, maybe pulling an IV loose, is all it takes to permanently imbed the image in your mind.

At least the recliner chairs are relatively comfortable. The quiet of the morning disturbed only by gentle conversation of others sharing the waiting game. The donor is rumored to be "in-house" (at UAB). And we wait. Finally, word comes from two new docs. One donor lung is available but may have some fluid in it. Not good news. Three doctors review the donor lung and my profile. Two out of three say okay; sadly that's not good enough. Transplant today a no-go. My first sense of serious disappointment renders me numb. Rapid nurse response follows. Unhook the EKG. Dislodge the IV needles. Rest in the chair and collect your thoughts. "So this is what it's like." Wow!

Calls of disheartenment were not unnoticeable in my voice. So where was the faith? Where was the trust in God? How could I get out of my own way and put God squarely in the center of this process? Susan and I decided to use this experience as our "dry run," having gained knowledge of what a potential organ recipient faces through the process; a knowledge filled with exhilaration that reminded of the first time I mastered the dinosaur keyboard of a Royal manual typewriter: a, s, d, f ... j, k, l, semi-colon. Home row keys. Some memories live forever. Understanding the process is not earth shaking but okay until next time. Nineteen hours passed. Today's ride is over. Now, my two diseased lungs and I sleep.

Reflection: One parenthood joy is seeing the look of wonderment on a baby's face; everything is new. So too the experience of transplant, an imperfect medical procedure offering hope where none existed. Life seems renewed. The agony of struggling to breathe ends. Joy interlocks with sadness; a life lost yet alive. I think of my donor often. Thanksgiving and Christmas 2010 brought tears. For some, the first year missing a loved one. For me, each September 28 evokes the same memory. A few believe you obtain another birthday to match your actual birth date. My reflection is a bit different: a stranger living in the body of a stranger. We take for granted mundane aspects of life. Donors change that image, giving recipients new hope. What constitutes our new and improved calling? "Why us," we question. Life revitalized, to what end? Does a transplant define life's meaning? What would you change? I can now answer that for myself. For Bob and Bill, and Shelia and Daisy, and Larry and Gail, thanks for taking the step with childlike wonder. With faith. With confidence. For all who share the experience of transplant, or consider the possibility at some unknown future date, you have an advocate and friend. Live on!

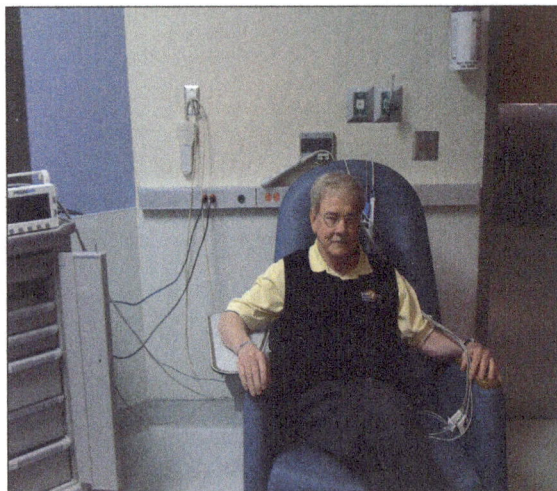

HTICU beginning to get initial
workup for possible transplant

CHAPTER 6

ANTICIPATION, EXULTATION, DEFLATION, GRITS

"Be pleased, O Lord, to deliver me! O Lord,
make haste to help me!"
Psalm 40:13

*H*eart palpitating. Excitement nearing crescendo. Transplant coming? Adrenalin boost rushing in with the second notification call. Familiarity bred from call #1. Completing a cycle every sixty seconds, the clock's minute hand rapidly approaches its smaller cousin tracking the hour. 1930 hours military time, 7:30pm CDT. Familiar ringtone signals the call of a UAB transplant coordinator. Thrill of anticipation provides metronome-like consistency to an elevated heartbeat. Only my second call, the routine feels familiar: #1. pack my overnight bag; #2. empty the medicine cabinet and stow my pills; #3. pack my cell phone (with its battery charger);

#4. computer with electric connectors? Nah! #5. man up through the weakness and drag my latest container(s) of supplemental oxygen. Excited cell call notification to family and friends proceeded as usual with prayer for the donor and his/her loved ones. The State of Alabama driver's license allows organ donor identification; always considered that a compassionate gesture. Aging organs probably not worthwhile at my moment of mortality but there's always research usage.

Today's world of confidentiality precludes revelation of donor information without express consent of those speaking on behalf of the donor. Sad in a way. Faceless and nameless stranger not knowing a recipient's joy at new life. Casual "thank you" fails the adequacy test for a life lost in exchange for a second-chance life. Natural human curiosity seeks knowledge about the donor's life: married, single, children, young (like a teen or early 20s), or older (40s and up), still working (at what occupation) or retired, hobbies, cause of death. Given time, we question.

Notes from my journal, June 6th and 7th "*. . .Ready for the day and church at 10:30. Rev. Charles Youngson and his staff (St. Thomas Episcopal, about 1 mile from our apartment) and congregation are very comforting and calming in our troubled waters.*"

7:15pm June 6, 2010 — *Lanier (transplant coordinator) called:* '*Mr. Godwin, we may have your lung. Be prepared for a long night.*' Educated guess from that last comment indicates the donor may not be nearby. My second time is a bit more familiar. Lanier commented that there are two lungs so if one doesn't work, there's a backup. Promising phone call. Our consumed evening meal already worked its way through our digestive systems. Feeling like veterans, with packed bags we journeyed to UAB after a phone call to Matthew, emails to our family and friends and a posting on CaringBridge. Phone calls to Wayne, sister Sue, Mike, Victor, Louise, Fr. Robert, Parker and Phyllis preceded our 8:00 pm UAB arrival. Louise's medical network filtered word that a transplant could be tonight. Preoccupied with anticipation I almost missed a friendly reminder from the HTICU nurse that plug-in to the hospital's main oxygen source was available "at our expense." I wonder where the generosity of "their expense" reflects itself on my six-figure bill. Nurse Claire from St. Paul's Episcopal Church in Mobile served as a kindly connection to our south Alabama homeland. Parker surprises with a late night visit to check on me and offer friendly relief for Susan, if needed. 11:00 pm already — three hours passed?

Dr. Keith Wille requested and received approval to utilize my type A+ blood donation for research. Smiley faces drawn with marker on my chest by Dr. Wille signified his appreciation for my donation. UAB *must* have a Godwin blood bank somewhere on campus. Understanding the process, the weekend wait shortens.

Prayerfully I move forward in faith. Remember Peter when doubt absorbed his thinking? When the rooster crowed? Stepping out of the boat and sinking because his faith sank? But Jesus reaches out for Peter and for me. He saves us when faith shakes like a 7.2 Richter scale earthquake. One step at a time I am called to follow; time after time my faith restored —

God never moves. When my faith wavers, God calls again and again. "Here I am, Lord, once more moving ahead in faith, resting in the comfort of your loving arms."

Moving to midnight – NPO means nothing to eat or drink, water included. Zero. Nada. Zilch. A short time expended for this lengthy journey, and again we wait. "You grace me, Lord, when I don't deserve your blessing, or so I think. Unearned is your grace and I am very thankful." The ticking clock moves forward to a new day; I move forward to a new life. I anticipate using my experiences and lessons learned to make it a more beneficial/fruitful life. Thanks Lord.

1:40am, June 7, 2010. Lindsay shaved me (mid-thigh to my neck) in preparation for surgery. Modesty now tossed from the window, partly as a result of age and partly as a result of who really cares? "We should have you ready by 2:00 am," quotes one of the nurses (do they ever sleep?). Staff movements generate greater urgency as the pace hurries toward surgery.

1:55am. We heard the O.R. crew was coming for me – one last stop at the men's room. OK, I'm ready. . . and the clock ticks . . .. and ticks . . . and I rest, waiting again.

3:30am. ticking time pauses as a familiar authority figure approaches my recliner. His foreboding facial expression needs no interpretation. "'The lungs are not good; you can get dressed and go home." Language delivered in tones as cutting as the surgical knife. Compassionate (this isn't his first time to be the messenger) but without flair or passion. Two words reverberate: not good. And like Peter, I sink – again! Quietly, quickly, efficiently removing apparatus from one of her patients, Lindsay's early morning workload reduces from three to two. Miss Piney Woods (AL) retrieves a wheelchair while Susan retrieves our car. Lindsay generates a long, soulful hug while helping load a sad, sorrowful patient into the front passenger seat. The second chapter of this transplant process now closes.

I think about my "humility checks" from God, and how this current discouragement of a lung transplant gone sour is the latest addition to my humility pile. Who did I think was in charge? A deserted U.S. Highway 280, eerily silent, signifies a quiet early Birmingham morning. Grits and an English muffin at our rental apartment serve as 4:15 am comfort food. Exhausted, depleted of energy, discouraged, Susan's singular patient appreciates her cuddling, loving arms and sleep comes quickly as we await another call. Numbness chills my soul. I don't know how or what to feel and we wait — again! Surely better times loom on the horizon — maybe. Third time a charm? Sense the shock.

Reflection: Try something once. If it doesn't work give it another chance. We are a nation of second-chancers. Transplant is different. One life has expended chances and another is receiving a second chance for life. All the garbage bagged in my memory seems insignificant when facing the possibility of passing from this life to the next. Mortality stares back from my mirror. Disappointment is modest, but present. Ever capture a prized stuffed toy from one of those carnival booth games? The moment turned sour when your prize is ripped from your arms by some inconsiderate young adult; reminiscent of my own youthful pranks. Disappointed? Surely you are. But transplant is life: a second chance to live. Some, to the dismay of transplant team members, accept the new lung and quickly succumb to the addictive influence of nicotine. A 40-year smoker, I understand the pull. But this is a second chance for life. Some seek the couch or recliner that is situated a remote control away from the cable access television. Exercise? Not on a lot of radars. Think of a second chance in your life. How have you responded? What have you learned? What purpose lies ahead? Use your second chance wisely. If an organ recipient, give honor to your donor's gift!

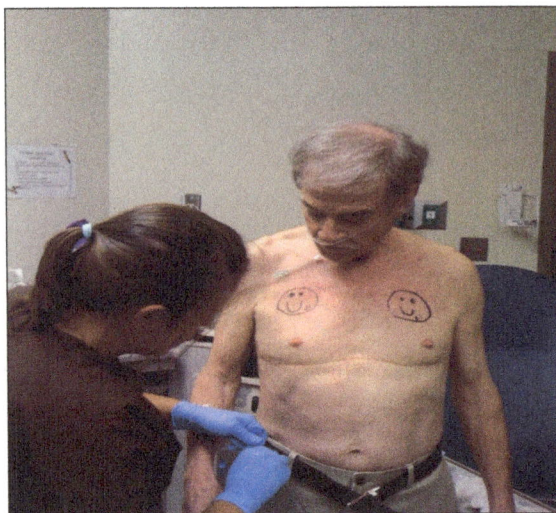

Dr. Wille's artwork on my chest

CHAPTER 7

FAITH, PATIENCE, WAITING

*"... do not be anxious about anything, but in everything,
by prayer and supplication, with thanksgiving,
let your requests be made known to God."*
Philippians 4:6

*W*ithdrawing from my memory bank, I recall faith, hope, love, these three abide but, with apologies to St. Paul, my greatest of these is — faith. Faith about God's presence throughout IPF pre-diagnosis, diagnosis, four-stent insertion left side of the heart, gaining entry to the coveted transplant waiting list, resettling to Birmingham, false alarms, fractured back, transplant surgery, recovery, heart attack, additional two-stent insertion, recovery again, and release back to reality. Faith that God would answer prayers in the manner we felt best for us. Faith that relinquishing control would allow God to perform His work without my attempt at interference. Faith that our 1,275 square foot corporate, two bedroom apartment would comfortably accommodate visiting guests while serving as Susan's workstation. Faith that daily excursions outside confining apartment walls would offer respite from occasional anxiety awaiting UAB's next call. Faith that oxygen tanks would fulfill their mission. Faith that God would honor fervent prayers offered daily for Susan and me. Faith that my buckled up, oxygen laden self would withstand the rigors of "wild" daily adventures. Want to know about wild? Visitations to Publix, Whole Foods, and Target, and Yogurt Mountain, and Starbucks, and Wal-Mart, and English Village, and Homewood, and Mountain Brook, the zoo and botanical gardens, and two-hundred-thirty-seven (who's counting) elegant residence filled side streets within a five-mile radius of our temporary home. Wild. Faith that "God's time" and mine would reveal compatibility. We live and believe faith's definition as ". . . the assurance of things hoped for but not yet seen." Faith.

And patient waiting. Wait. Be patient. Wait some more. "Give me patience please Lord, and give it to me **now!**" Waiting became standard for our Birmingham time and wisely we decided to bloom where planted. Meanwhile, the nagging inner voice: "When would we have THE phone call?" "Be patient," offered the thought in my mind. Wait some more. Don't forget faith.

Experiencing patient waiting, we gaze through the camera's lens, viewing the terrain of the three mountains which comprise a loose definition of the metropolitan Birmingham area. Intriguing mountain views for those who normally live near sea level. Distressed breathing issues were enhanced by Birmingham's hilly terrain and higher elevation. Exhaustion was frequently experienced. "More oxygen," screamed my body seeking relief from a constant companion – the "elephant" size tank. Gritted teeth and under-the-breath expletives betray my frequent agitation at settling the tank into the car. With diminished arm strength, manipulation of the oxygen cart can be compared to single handedly hanging wallpaper. Tubing draped back seat to front occasionally entangled in the headrest. Major coordination involved. Separate the seat belt, oxygen hoses, and headrest. "This new life is really great Lord, just great. Thanks." Sarcastic gratitude.

Susan's faith and inner strength sustained my life companion. Maintaining vigilant watch over my activities, God's special angel endured additional crisis when I fell in our apartment. Can you say L3 compression fracture? Thankfully, the Rocky Ridge Fire and Rescue Department was one quarter mile away. Diagnosis, treatment, and a ride to the UAB Emergency Room all swiftly accomplished. First question to the ER doc: "can I have a painkiller?" Immediately on the heels of his affirmative response, another inquiry: "With this fracture am I still eligible for lung transplant?" "Is this guy for real," questioned one of the on-duty ER doctors. Yep! Tears tickled moisturized cheeks as the doctor affirmed my continued eligibility for transplant. Thank you Lord.

Comforting an already physically impaired husband, Susan never missed a beat as president and chief visionary officer of Christian Copyright Solutions (CCS), the company God entrusts to her leadership and care. Dealing with churches and non-profit organizations nationwide, her laptop and cell phone proved a dynamic pair of lifelines for constant communication with clients and staff. Can you say "virtual office?" Strength aside, sometimes she just needed a yogurt. Private tears occasionally escaped my gaze though I was aware that her suffering, both physically and emotionally, compared to what I was enduring. Visits from family and friends allowed Susan the luxury of time away from her #1 patient waiting the call for a new lung. R-r-r-ing. R-r-r-ing. R-r-r-ing. "Transplant time?"

Ultimately, the rewards of patient waiting led to transplant and the humorous aspects of response to call #6. Rest assured, those who endure family crisis know times of laughter are infrequent. My journal contains numerous references to St. Peter and his denials of Jesus and his lack of faith. Remember the denials? Not once. Not twice. Three times and all before the rooster announced day's dawning. Peter's response took him outdoors where he wept bitterly. Peter's weakened faith and lack of trust so resembling our spiritual failures today. Does recognition of those failures cause bitter weeping?

My story, though, isn't about the physical and emotional suffering Susan and I endured. The story reflects the strength of faith, constantly affirmed by family, friends, and strangers. Faith withstanding the onslaught of negativity as time and again patience severely tested. "You're too old." "You're too weak for transplant." "Those heart arteries are too blocked." "Type II diabetics don't normally get new lungs." "What about that fractured back?" Naysayers crumble your defenses at every turn. "Help Lord. Help us survive and grow with the love of Your Son comforting every step of the way." His response? A personal visit, card, email, or phone call happening each time the naysayer's "no" was outgaining His "yes." God's time.

Expressions of support, in multiple forms, arrived courtesy of "angel mail." As the beautiful writing "One Set of Footprints" reminds, God loves us dearly. When we feel abandoned and alone, then He carries us. Faith and patience. God's angels raised us from the miry pit of this miraculous journey. Decent physical shape belies my spotty health history: type II diabetes, IPF both lungs, four stent insertion on my heart's left side, heart attack, and two stent insertion on heart's right side, fall and fracture of my L3 vertebrae and, oh yes, a left lung transplant. Blink in amazement at the miracle of my survival. I do. Survival attributed to incredible circumstances, so say some negative-ites. Maybe these words and reflections can change that thinking. My experience changed me and impacts others. Feeling separated from God? He does not move. He loves each of His children. Love Him, too.

Reflection: Go to the movies. Scan the service counter for the shortest line. Enticing aromas of freshly puffed kernels of corn, overflowing edges of the metal kettle. Pop, pop-pop, pop-pop-pop, pop-pop-pop-pop-pop . . . Experience a taste sensation of corn meshing with butter and salt flavorings. Five young teens join their friend awaiting service just two patrons ahead in line. Now you've retreated to number eight in line. Patience about to expire. Christmas crowd? Sixteen service lines open to accommodate. Do you always pick the wrong one? Patience. "Next year I won't wait until Christmas Eve." Right. Are you a patient driver or a "bumper sitter?" Yellow caution light cause you to put the pedal to the metal? What lesson have you learned from a lack of patience? Does it really matter to wait an additional fifty-seven seconds because the light is red? What impact this slight delay cause in the hours remaining in your day? What if God's patience level with us resembles our patience with others? Remember, faith is the assurance of things not yet seen. Wait patiently.

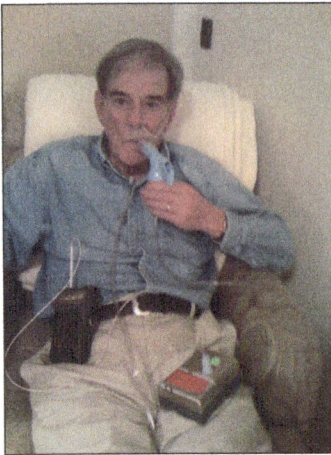

Transplant acceptability
week long testing –
March 2010

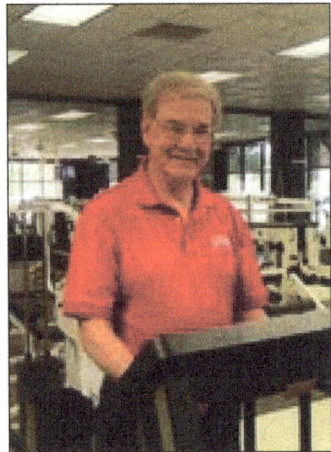

Fitness Center
Member of the
Month – May 2011

CHAPTER 8

THE CROSS, GIFTS, RELATIONSHIPS

"Each one must give as he has decided in his heart,
not reluctantly or under compulsion for
God loves a cheerful giver."
II Corinthians 9:7

*C*ards. E-mails. Social media postings. Phone calls.
Personal visits. Material gifts. Family. Friends.
Strangers. Angel communication signaled awareness that
someone, somewhere, ushered prayers heavenward on our
behalf. Frequently we sensed prayer partners. Susan, me, our
unknown donor and his/her loved ones, all neatly wrapped
together with faith in the Trinity.

Surprise. An unexpected gift from Susan brings profound
comfort and peace. I commend for your consideration the
gift of a Palm Cross for a prayer vessel during times of tribula-
tion and thanksgiving. Initial praying hands laid upon this
cross belonged to Dr. Victor J. Thannickal, UAB's Pulmonary

Division Director. Completing the circle of prayer were Dr. Thannickal's staff members and a physician in the middle of her recruiting process. Research friend Dr. Louise Hecker turned from her mice and microscope to enlist as an early member of the "cross brigade." Hand carved from walnut, the cross creations contain no finish. "Natural oils in human skin," declares the artisan, "provide the cross's finish." Unique idea. Sharing time with the cross, encourage caregivers (family, friends, hospital personnel) to pray (silently or aloud) for the patient, the donor family, for transplants and all entrusted with patient care.

Arrival of my transplant hour, with summons to the surgical suite via gurney transport, proved to be the only time the cross left my side. Otherwise, sleepless nights? Half-opened eyes, in a slumbered fog, searched the ever present tray table for my comforting cross. Placement on my heart preceded a prayer of thanks for hands that had prayed over that cross. Sleep deprivation vanished. Pain? Same regimen, same results. No doubting the strength of comfort available from the cross during my preparation time, surgery, recovery, recuperation, and renewal of normal life.

The autographed fooftball? A post transplant visit brought face-moistening tears which flowed freely when son Matthew (he prefers Matt) presented his gift. The autographed St. Luke's High School football showing a final score of St. Luke's 38, A.L. Johnson 12. The Wildcats' initial victory ending a winless streak in their first year of competition. Prominent position on the football's face belonged to St. Luke's coaching staff member Coach Matt. Autographed: "I love you dad, Matthew."

Beginning operation in 2009, St. Luke's Episcopal High School in Mobile offered Coach Matt various coaching opportunities. During formative years, as a ten year attendee at St. Luke's (pre-kindergarten to 8th grade), Matthew the active sports enthusiast played any sport available to him. Coaching high school football presented new challenges and opportunities. With two wins in their first year program, the St. Luke's Wildcats did not enjoy huge success. Two wins. The meaningful one for Coach Matt and his dad proved to be the victory over A. L. Johnson. As a first win following some pummeling defeats, the football represented a spirit of not quitting, not giving up. I still hear that inner voice: "Definitely do not lose faith in what you are trying to accomplish."

Third major surprise from a totally unexpected source; the Gautier (MS) First United Methodist Church Prayer Quilt Ministry Team. Little did I expect the gift of a beautiful, handmade quilt. Inscribed on the artwork's back side, "This quilt was made for Gary Godwin with love, hope, and prayers." Thanks to my unmet friend Larry and wife Mary Jane. Lots of communication between Larry's Gautier, MS home and me though we traveled two divergent transplant hospital roads. UAB you know was my choice. Larry discovered Ochsner in New Orleans a closer fit from his home in south Mississippi. Transformed, we are transplant buddies. Larry and Mary Jane share a history with us, though we have yet to share time together.

Brief quilt background. During a phone call, Larry sensed growing discontent in my voice. Still, the query seemed unusual. "What's your street address in Birmingham?" Correspondence normally transpired through emails or occasional phone calls. "Maybe he's sending a get well card" I reasoned. Seven days after providing address information, an angel mail package arrived from Gautier. Stunned at the package contents, tears gently glistened my cheeks as I read the significance of every bright blue bow stitched on the quilt: "Each knot represents a prayer that was said for you." And I know NONE of these people, which makes no difference. Adorning my office, that quilt evokes proud memories of Matthew's pre-school artwork. More than excellent stitchery, the quilt represents the love of strangers on their life mission of sharing with other strangers. Another group of God's angels, doing His work on Earth.

Bouncing to Birmingham from the Mitchell Center, on the University of South Alabama (USA) campus in Mobile, came an autographed basketball from Head Coach Ronnie Arrow and USA's Jaguar team. Serving as home court advantage, the 10,000 seat multi-purpose Mitchell Center opened in 1999, becoming one of the finest basketball venues in the country. Concurrently, my public address (p.a.) career began anew as we dribbled past the 1900's. Later breathing difficulties did not deter my resolve. Thankfully, announcing duties blended into my brief, almost staccato, style. Reporting on-court action, my lungs gasped for breath. Normally, p.a. duties bounced from the basketball court to the baseball diamond.

One decade into the 2000's, my sports year crashed like a falling star.

Long time USA buddies Joel (Athletic Director), Joe (former A.D.) and Hal, (Associate A.D.) were three pioneers of basketball wars waged at "The Mitch." Joel and Hal, basketball game day production coordinators, feeding info to the p.a. announcer (me). Working with this trio evoked visions of the three musketeers. With Joe's retirement and Joel's return as USA's top athletics leader, the Mitchell Center alliance returned. Sadly missing the 2010 baseball season as p.a. guy brought assurances from the top that "the microphone awaits your return."

Saddled by illness or injury, anticipation of future events brings comfort. Despite health issues keep on fighting for satisfaction of a joyful goal. For me, reservation of the p.a. seat and microphone proved one more incentive to fight and defeat this lung destroying disease. Anticipation of a new lung diminished the fear of climbing the eighteen steps from the Mitchell Center to the parking lot. Small victories count. Thanks to Joel, Hal, and Joe for unwavering support.

Reflection: Think of a favorite toy from preschool years. Maybe you were three or four. Can you remember? Or birthday or Christmas gifts from five years earlier. Anything come to mind? Now, think of a favorite relative, no longer on an earthly pilgrimage. What makes him or her stand out? "Things" in life wither and rust and decay, often relegated to attic storage and forgotten. Sound familiar? Have you checked your attic recently? Real treasures in this life evolve from relationships with God's children like Larry and Ronnie and Joel and Hal and Joe and the Gautier First United Methodist Church Prayer Quilt Ministry Team. Relationships take time. The effort proves invaluable. Which friend, or stranger, is on your list for conversation this week? Nobody? Start the list. Taking the time probably produces two happy hearts. While processing this final first edit, happy news flowed from a dear friend. Her father and brother put aside past differences and enjoyed a powerfully heartfelt, emotional reunion that bridged the chasm of multiple years' separation. Somebody extended the peaceful hand of forgiveness. Relationships prove their value.

Prayer quilt from Gautier
MS United Methodist Church
P.A. guy returns to his Jaguar seat

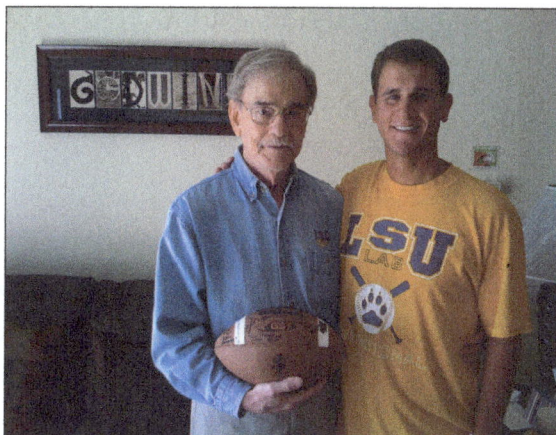

Game ball from St. Luke's High 1st football win

CHAPTER 9

THIRD TIME NOT SO CHARMING

". . . we rejoice in our sufferings, knowing that suffering
produces endurance and endurance produces
character and character produces hope. . ."
Romans 5: 3-4

*T*he rhythmic noise sounds familiar. Disturbing our peaceful evening's quiet, the modular desk phone beckons, hopefully UAB calling. Transplant time routine begins anew. "This is UAB Transplant for Mr. Godwin. We may have a lung for you. Please don't eat or drink anything and be here (HTICU) as soon as possible."

Hot, muggy June 24, 2010, our day 33 in Birmingham. Last call for transplant occurred June 6, 2010. Mind and body a bit feisty, testing the virtue of patience. My first two calls produced UAB visits within fourteen days of our Birmingham arrival. Spoiled? No question. A degree of entitlement brought kingly expectations. "Where's my lung?" Push God all you want. Don't be surprised when He pushes back.

Fifteen plus minutes away along US Highway 280 we follow signs to University Boulevard. Pass St. Vincent's Hospital, head to 1802 6th Avenue South, thank the driver (Susan), grab oxygen tank and cart, step lively to the elevator. Welcome once again to UAB's medical facility. My 5th floor destination determined by a singular finger punch. Susan finds a parking space in the 4th Avenue parking garage. Slowly maneuvering quiet, almost silent hallways, oxygen tank in tow, I find the night-shift charge nurse offering welcoming words: "Mr. Godwin, we've been expecting you." Into the HTICU "prep room" I await the routine of a blood bank donation, blood pressure, weight, pulse, oxygen saturation level, temperature, and hookup to the hospital's oxygen supply (to save my tanks). Semi-reclined in the UAB HTICU version of a lounger/recliner, I anticipate the needle's insertion into a receptive vein not prone to roll. Primary purpose of donations to the Godwin blood bank? Fulfillment of the requirements necessary to ensure my donor's blood type and mine are a perfect match; only perfection works for this staff dedicated to the preservation of donor organs. One striking feature of tonight's room — none of the usual overhead lighting. A darkened room lit solely by indirect, under cabinet lighting proved to be an omen of the evening. A short evening.

Susan's late night footsteps on a quiet hospital unit floor closely follow the departing footsteps of the messenger and his unwelcome news. "Mr. Godwin, we tried to call you. We're sorry, but the lungs are not good. We can't give you a transplant tonight." Thankfully, the vein seeking, blood sucking had yet to begin. Regardless, this time was different. I had become spoiled to the frequency of phone calls, hoping the next one would lead to transplant. I readied myself. Donors were available. Why couldn't I get a good lung? Disappointed. Dejected. Deterred. There was no joy in Birmingham. Poor little Gary had struck out. Pity party time, mixed with a dollop of anger. Thoughts and reactions improperly transmitted to Susan, my biggest supporter. "Careful buddy. She's the only constant in your life right now." One positive resulted from tonight's rejection. The parking garage gives you thirty minutes free parking. We qualified. Yippee.

Disappointment of the evening emotionally shared with nurse Lindsay. She who shaved and otherwise prepped me for the second call which we surely felt was leading to transplant, only to be deferred to another day. We discovered later that Lindsay also felt saddened by this evening's news. Sweet, young professional with one final opportunity for kindness — pushing my wheelchair to the garage. Lindsay's consoling words and sorrowful goodbye hug sent Susan and her patient quietly into Birmingham's late night.

Recollection of this memorable and yet forgettable day from my journal, June 24, 2010: "*6.24.10. Quiet morning. Susan had a less than perfect night (no details are necessary but she had a very bad night). Sure hope it's a soon-to-be-passing bug working out of her system. May need to cancel Fr. Robert's (our priest at home church in Daphne, AL) visit later. My escape is to the store. Need some supplies and tummy-soothing medicine for my sweetie.*

8:05pm - PHONE CALL #3 . . . Fr. Robert is on his way (to our apartment). We waited for him, said our prayers, packed our bags, and headed to UAB with Robert expected to follow shortly. Once again, the "rush" of the moment got me in a hyper state so thankfully Susan felt good enough to drive. We've been (to UAB) so many times we know the acceptable entrance and elevator location. Our routine? I go to HTICU, Susan parks the car. Young Lindsay is on duty tonight; it's good to see each other again. As I recline in my now-familiar lounger while awaiting Susan, the charge nurse seeks and finds me.

Soulful eyes reflect an inner spirit. I detect forthcoming news won't make me happy. "Antigens don't match. Well, I'm sorry." Short trip this time. Susan arrives to hear the news, and we head home before the car engine has cooled. Always seeking some positive from any situation, I realize our parking garage fee is non-existent. About the only happiness from this visit which otherwise leaves us dejected, disappointed, discouraged, downhearted, disheartened. Lots of "d" words and frustration. Ride home is silent. Emotionally spent again and Susan is still not feeling well. Back home it's mindless TV: (1) the news; (2) Tonight show; and (3) bedtime. A few phone calls, then emails, and a CaringBridge posting. Romans 5:3-4, Romans 5:3-4. Courage and perseverance and again we wait!

One quick addendum. The charge nurse bringing the "no go" news was not as abrupt as my notes indicate. Very professional, delivering unhappy news to a patient anticipating lung transplant. Theirs is not an easy job. I came to know and respect many in the HTICU for the manner in which they handle difficult situations; and every situation is difficult, especially the cases indicating denial of a lung transplant. For me, the evening's anticipation blew away like the ashen residue from a charcoal fire.

Third time as some believe was NOT the charm. And it's only been a month, for heaven's sake. "OK God, where are you? I'm growing a bit weary and more than a little agitated. Aren't you alongside? What's the problem? I'm ready. Let's get this transplant behind us!" A priest told me long ago it's okay to be angry with God. He can handle our agitation. Self serving selfishness produced no "thank you" for today. No "thank you" for today's trials and tribulations of the Godwin family. No sensation of the presence of the Lord. And guess who moved? Wavering faith disappoints me, and I believe God probably wasn't too happy either. Thrusting my anger on Him, I demand upfront information about the next call. His immediate response came in "angel mail" received June 25th, the day after my third call.

One of God's angels from northwest Florida penned these words: "May the peace of God rule in your hearts as you continue this glorious journey of waiting. What a privilege to wait. I pray you will know the Father's heartbeat for you and His people as He holds you close. With quiet trust I wait with you. It is a joy." You too, Brooke, are a joy. A new perspective on waiting — a glorious journey. Wow. With a helping hand lifting us out of the muck and mire, the disappointment of call #3 becomes a distant memory. A troubling surprise awaits with a dicey donor, our fourth call. "Many more surprises, Lord?"

Reflection: Not much to reflect. In and out of UAB before the parking space expended our free minutes. My major reflection shown above resounds frequently for Susan and me ". . . this glorious journey of waiting." Patient waiting disappears from many vocabularies. Speaking of disappearing, I'd love to disappear from the IPF death row awaiting execution. Agitation and frustration become commonplace in the arena of transplant waiting. Look upon waiting as a "glorious journey." Easy? Thinking "outside the box" seldom comes easily. Do you wait with patience, or anger? Where do you wait and for what do you wait? In the grocery line? Bank? Doctor's office? Dry cleaners? Red traffic light? Does that fifty-seven second wait for color changes from red to green really destroy your day? Breakfast, lunch, dinner served daily at precisely the same time, or do you wait? Does the school bus arrive with television news show punctuality? For you, is waiting a "glorious journey?" If not, next time you wait, challenge yourself to exhibit patience. Change your thought process and change your world. Wait patiently. Endurance, character, and hope will surely follow.

Transplant coordinators & HTICU nurses
= special angels

Chapter 10

Four Finds Faith's
Flame Flickering

*"Blessed are those who hunger and thirst for
righteousness, for they shall be satisfied."*
Matthew 5:6

OK. So it's been six weeks. Waiting. Patiently (or not patiently) waiting. First two calls within a week of my Birmingham arrival provided a sense of superiority. "I'm ready, so let's go." Not that simple. Schedule a doctor's appointment and receive a definitive date and time. Not so with transplantation. Be near a phone at all times, everywhere you go. And I do mean *everywhere!* Well, maybe not the shower, but almost everywhere. Pack your overnight bag. Move quickly at a moment's notice. Inhibit your food and beverage intake. Light meals serve a dual purpose. You don't know the hour when "the" call comes so at all times, be ready.

Like bees building a hive, buzzy activity abounds prior to arrival at your transplant center. Mentally and physically, traveling through your personal twilight zone, be prepared. My mind and spirit speed past ready for transplant surgery. The wait between the third and fourth calls seemed incredibly long; June 24th to August 4th. Forget the fact that UAB was well ahead of schedule with my four lung offerings. Oh, and don't forget the fact that your transplant team awaits a donor match as perfect as possible.

Patience? Mine began to wane long ago. Questions of doubt made me feel like Thomas: "Show me the nail holes, Lord!" Questions. "Had I been forgotten? Was my name no longer hovering near the top of the waiting list? Facing abbreviated number of days, was my time so short I moved down on the waiting list?" Multiple questions grasp command of your senses. "OK God, where are you? Why won't you give me a healthy lung? Are you mad at me? Ready to transform me into submission to your will? Telling me I won't get a lung? What's going on, Lord?"

My questions showed an increasing sense of irritability. "Who am I to be treated like this?" Quite a brazen question, wouldn't you agree? But I asked, just as any family asks the same question about a parent, sibling, or other close relative facing a difficult disease and its effects. Questions without apparent answers arrive in droves. Patience with the transplant process proceeds on thin ice. Whoops. How thin? The chilling news of call #4 likened to falling through a crack in the ice floe. Cold. Very cold.

Susan and I retrace steps of a familiar routine. Pack the bags. Include pills in the shaving kit. Susan drives. I ride, making phone calls to family and friends. She deposits me at the hospital front entrance and parks the car in the 4th street parking lot. Compassionate greeting (as usual) from HTICU staff on duty. For how many reasons can the transplant team say "no?" Listen to just a few. "Blood type doesn't match." "Antigens don't share compatibility." "The lung we wanted to transplant has some excess fluid." "There are early signs of emphysema." "The donor lived too far from the transplant center, and the lung did not survive travel." Susan and I were not surprised by numerous suggested reasons for lack of transplant. A new reason to refuse transplant, however, did stun our sensibilities.

"Mr. Godwin," declared the doctor, "you need to know that the donor had a high-risk lifestyle." What does that mean? Alcohol? Drugs? Excessive tobacco use? Sexual promiscuity? HIV positive? Hepatitis C? Any other addictions?" No response; patient confidentiality you know. Not knowing the donor, Susan and I spent a few minutes of worthless supposition. So many prayers seemingly answered; tonight, I'm the only patient called for this transplant possibility. The decision relinquished by doctors and delivered to husband and wife. "Why don't you make it a little tougher, Lord? We ask for a healthy donor, you give us a 'high-risk profile' donor. Thanks a lot!"

Frustrated? Right. Agitated? Right again. Anxious? A new sensation creeps in. Why would medical professionals think I wanted to take this risk? I'm already a 'high-risk patient' due to age and other medical issues. "OK Gary. Get past the emotions and make a decision. Now." "Mr. Godwin, the UAB plane is on the airport tarmac, waiting to retrieve the lung if you want it." If I want it. Listed for transplant on May 5th, receiving three prior calls to come to the hospital for possible transplant and now it's up to Susan and me. Fr. Robert, help.

A late night call to our priest begs the question "what are your thoughts? Take it or leave it?" Faith alive through long distance prayer brings comfort and we request the presence of the nearby transplant team members. Holding hands to form a circle of prayer, the team members feel the Spirit's presence as I listen to Fr. Robert's prayer of intercession. Termination of the long distance call brought this comment from one of the doctors: "Mr. Godwin, we'll give you and your wife a few moments alone to make a decision," states the pulmonologist. *Make a life-altering decision, and you've got precious seconds to devise an answer.* With complete faith that God is in our presence, both alone and with our medical team, the decision makes itself.

August 4, 2010. 10:40pm. "Mr. Godwin," the physician inquires, "the plane is ready to go. Are you Yes or No?" "Thanks, but no thanks. Family, friends and strangers have been praying for a "perfect lung," and we don't believe this is the answer." Words so difficult came so easily. One question did get answered. "Why would anyone want a potentially damaged lung?" I inquired. "For some," said the doctor, "this is a last hope and they are willing to take the risk." Had my lifespan become so diminished that this option should even be considered? Scary, very scary. Calliope on the merry-go-round inspires notes below penned into my journal.

August 4, 2010: *Hump Day. Inside exercise was a 7 minute walk in the apartment. Outside? Travel to Wal-Mart. Whoopee !!*

6pm Healing and Eucharist service at St. Thomas, especially mindful of donors. (Semi-regulars at the 6:00 pm service, Susan and I felt need for healing prayer).

7:15pm Exercise at the apartment complex fitness center.

7:45pm Lanier (transplant coordinator) called. "We may have a lung; be ready"

8:15pm Lanier says to come to UAB for possible transplant.

8:30pm We headed to HTICU, after phone calls to family and friends.

8:50pm Arrival at UAB meant more x-rays and massive donation for the Godwin blood bank. Had a call from research scientist and new friend Dr. Louise Hecker. Working late tonight, she will keep Susan company if needed.

10:40pm UAB jet waiting to retrieve donor lung. By the way, Dr. Leon says donor has a "high-risk lifestyle." Do you want the lung, yes or no? Called Fr. Robert for prayer. "Not this time." Ugh. Charles Gary Godwin

Diverting attention from ourselves and our frustrations we finally allowed God to participate in our process. How noble of us. "Sorry it took so long Lord. Thank you for never leaving us. By the way, is there a new lung available? You still produce miracles right? How did you turn that water into wine at the wedding feast?"

Journal notes dated August 5, 2010, the day after call #4.

"A day of recovery. Lot of caring notes and expressions of support through emails and CaringBridge. Spoke with Lanier. I am a good size for transplant but not a lot of good luck lately. Lanier did say the UAB plane was on the tarmac last night waiting for our decision. Wow! Other times in an earlier life I would have reveled in the power and control I could exert. Last night the sensation was one of inconveniencing a lot of folks including transplant surgeon Dr. McGiffin and the pilot. Exercise at night highlights an otherwise quiet day. Thanks for God's presence in many ways today. Strengthening my commitment to Him becomes critical. Gary

"What's next Lord?" Three people waiting for one of two lungs. Uh oh. Who, if anybody, gets the short straw? Is there always such drama with transplant?

 ***Reflection:*** If I thought call #3 was difficult due to quickness, it turned to baby pablum compared to this one. "Lord, just let me take charge for a little while. I can handle

it." I'm confident God laughed heartily. "Sure Gary," I can hear him say. "Every day I give you options," His voice booms. "And," He continued, "every day you make choices. Some good. Some not so good. But go ahead. This time around, you make the choice. Not so easy is it?" Yet one more humility check. Every day He allows us to make choices. Maybe not as complex as lung transplant donor suitability, but choices. He provides parameters such as the Ten Commandments of Old Testament and the love of neighbor and self in the New Testament. Today, what choices confront you? What will guide your decisions? Will you proceed in faith or in fear? Choices. Maybe, just maybe, you don't want to be in charge after all.

Father Robert post transplant visit

CHAPTER 11

HEART TO HEART

*"A friend loves at all times and a brother
is born for adversity."*
Proverbs 17:17

~

*C*ardiologist. Life saver-extender. Gentle. Learned. One of God's angels. Dedicated to the healing profession. Doc with a sense of humor. Twice, my life relied on the surgical expertise of Dr. Vijay Misra. April 12, 2010, prearranged surgery called for two-stent insertion around my heart. Addition to the lung transplant waiting list hinged on Dr. Misra's success. Multiple votes of affirmation situated my heart in excellent hands.

Knowing an incredible health history, Dr. Misra called upon all his resources to ensure my healthiest heart possible for lung transplant. Two-stent insertion doubled to four stents. The complexity of multiple health circumstances carried additional difficulties for the surgery. Maintaining a degree of awareness, I could share unusual circumstances with Dr. Misra while undergoing the procedure. Sometime during the operation I felt it necessary to explain what I considered a medical difficulty. "Dr. Misra," "Mr. Godwin, do not talk." "But Dr. Misra," "Mr. Godwin, please do not talk." "Dr. Misra, briefly, I'm experiencing some chest pains and I think you should be aware." Calming jangled nerves his response: "I know. I'm causing them." My immediate thought? "Well, stop it." Turns out, Dr. Misra's expansion of the arterial opening for stent insertion produced the pain. Not funny then, the pain becomes more humorous with age.

September 30, 2010 marked my second opportunity for Dr. Misra's work. Recovering from transplant surgery, I awakened with serious chest pains. Heart attack. By God's grace, an on-duty Dr. Misra provided rapid surgical repair with two more stents. Having a heart attack? No better place to be than a hospital's Intensive Care Unit. Sadly, tragically, Dr. Misra's cardiology days have ended. Completely unexpected, he passed away in the summer of 2011 at the age of 51. A heartbreaking loss for UAB, his department, and patients. With a joyful place in my heart and the hearts of many others, thank you and God's peace Dr. Vijay Misra.

Reflection: *Each day presents a wonderful gift from our heavenly Father. Treat those days thankfully, accepting each one with joy and gratitude.*

CHAPTER 12

I SURRENDER

*"And we know that for those who love God all things
work together for good, for those who are called
according to His purpose."*
Romans 8:28

One, two, three. One donor. Two lungs. Three people awaiting lung transplant. Let's see: two divided by three; isn't that a fraction? Is it allowable to transplant fractions? Waiting in our usual spot, HTICU, this trip includes two strangers sharing similar needs. One man, one woman, two caregivers, Susan and me. Three victims with diminishing lung capacity suck the generous supply of UAB oxygen in the prep room. Flashback recalls multiple compact, one bedroom apartments rented during my college life. Happy memories from a happier lifetime generate visible signs of joy. Returning to reality, as realization of circumstances struck, I shuddered in a meager attempt to stifle tears. If transplant takes place, at least one of our trio goes home empty — again! "Lord, I want you to help my friends but what about me? I need a lung too. Much as I feel sorry for them, I NEED A LUNG!" Feeling like Sammy Selfish I want God to answer my prayer the way I want my prayer answered. Even had I known the surprises awaiting this day, my selfish self desired God's favor.

Spiritual brother Mike pushes the gas pedal of his BMW to the legal speed limits of I-65, Birmingham bound from Fairhope for a mini visit. Susan gratefully accepts a well deserved pass from caregiver responsibilities. A good time awaits us all.

8.19.10 journal entry: *"SPECIAL TREAT!!! Mike is coming for a visit. Breakfast and morning prayer went before a grocery stop at Target. Lunch precedes a 50-minute treadmill and weight workout. Treadmilling at 3 miles per hour, 20 pounds on each forearm.*

8:15pm. "Don't eat or drink anything. We may call you for transplant." The familiar call from UAB transplant! Mike and I had just arrived at our neighborhood frozen yogurt store. Presented the opportunity, he would witness the transplant process from the beginning. With a potential lung awaiting we never got the yogurt. Movie watching, Susan abandoned the final ten minutes and met us at the apartment. Balance sheet: I owe Mike one yogurt, Susan one movie.

8:30pm. Report to HTICU at UAB.

Arrival in the HTICU prep room, we noted three in waiting for two lungs.

H-m-m-m-m-m. All of us enjoying the UAB oxygen supply. My young friend Lindsay is on duty again tonight . . . And Andy is in charge.

10:30pm Mike and Susan in house. Three wait for two lungs. Do any make it tonight?

10:33pm Andy says the donor is in the house. My heart beats a few ticks faster.

11:15pm (Rev.) Charles Youngson is in the house, joining the prep room assemblage.

8.20.10 arrives and at 12:20am Charles offers anointing and prayers on the Palm Cross, with prayers for healing offered to all roommates. And Susan and Mike and Charles and me finish with the Lord's Prayer as we all hold hands and commend my care to the Lord. And Charles drifted silently into the good night.

1:25am Andy brings the news we did not want to hear. Dr. Young says the lungs are no good. "Let's get vital signs, take out the IV's and send you home." One more time.

OK, so we wait again. Nothing new. We're getting acclimated. Memory bank recalls faithful strength of finishers who never quit and quitters who never finish. Type II diabetic. IPF sufferer. 4-stents on the left side of the heart. And no new lung. "Lord, you've given me quite enough. This whole process is getting mighty old. How about some different action?" Uh-Oh! Be careful what you ask for because . . . I got some different action alright. The fall of the Gary continues my surrender —finally! *Charles Gary Godwin*

Reflection: Think about Christmas. Consider your next birthday. When is your wedding anniversary? Start date for SEC football? Post time for the Kentucky Derby? When is hunting season? March Madness? Date and time for your next doctor appointment? Specific dates indicate those special times. Disruption of plans accompanies illness or injury. Preparations get put on hold. How often? Until we recover and expectations of upcoming fun and joyful events pump new spring in our steps. Considering the life altering action of organ transplant, make plans judiciously for a specific time. Maintain flexibility in your life schedule. Phone call indicating this might be the time presents smiles and happier attitudes. Lots of joy in life dashed to pieces when plans go astray. And what is your response to life's lemons? Joyful plans placed on hold, or eliminated, bring anger, disappointment, frustration, disgust? Patience, people, patience. During difficult times, angered emotions and frustrated feelings overcome almost all other sensations. Recall that everything is possible with God. Need any proof? Look at me.

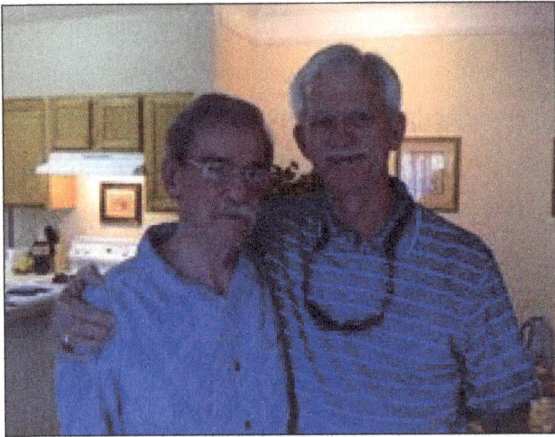

Spiritual brother Mike

CHAPTER 13

FORGIVENESS, PRAYER, DON, LYNN, & CLAIRE

$\iff$

"for all who honor us with their prayers"

$\mathcal{D}$ ay 109. **Journal notes from September 9th:** *"My dear friends - Your words touch the deepest parts of my heart, releasing emotions rarely shown to others. Were you here at this moment, you'd be feeding me tissues to absorb the moisture of my tears. On days of anguish (like our unlisted home phone ringing – hoping for UAB – getting a telemarketer) I'll receive a card, email, CaringBridge note or some expression of love from one of you and realize how much you bless me.*

Sometime I have probably agitated the heck out of you. I have definitely evoked God's anger. A lifelong memory expression is a plea for God to '… not weigh my merits, but pardon my offenses' … a large reason why a favorite reference is Luke 6:36: '… be merciful just as your Father is merciful.'

Never before appeared the vision of this unknown life journey. I am humbly grateful for all who keep Susan and me part of their regular prayer life. God has placed you in my life for many reasons. The vulnerability of this illness brings closeness to mortality I never expected to experience in my 60s. But we don't walk alone; there is a strong sense of your closeness. Thanks for staying with us.

Christian singer-songwriter Lynn DeShazo and our priest from Montrose AL, Fr. Mark DiCristina, turned our modest apartment into a sanctuary yesterday as we worshipped, sang, and shared the Lord's Supper. What an exquisite reminder that '... whenever two or three are gathered in My name, I will be in the midst of them.' And Jesus was, and is, and will be. Through His grace, you are my beloved family and friends and I am humbly thankful." Gary

My surrender continues. Notes to loved ones indicate I've relinquished control and sent it back to where it always resided. And God laughs heartily. Call #4 He let me have control. Based on circumstances, I quickly returned that hot potato. Seemingly easy decisions weigh heavier on our spirits than anticipated. Prayer sustains. Offering thanks for so many seems insignificant with the words "thank you." Somewhere, the word exists with the appropriate vowels and consonants to fully express thanks but I don't know its existence. Meantime, with permission from Don Moen and Claire Cloninger, listen to the prayerful words of our journey and accept our thanks for all who pray for us constantly.

"SOMEBODY'S PRAYING FOR ME"
Don Moen & Claire Cloninger

"I was lost in a desert land ... So dry and thirsty ...
But God was there where he'd always been ...
Giving grace and mercy ...
So hard to sing and hard to pray ...Yet I knew
His word was true ...
And then one day my faith returned ...And suddenly
I knew ...
Somebody's praying for me ... Somebody's
knocking on Heaven's door ....
Somebody's praying for me ... Somebody's lifting
me up to the Lord ...
I knew it had to be ... Somebody down
on their knees ...
Somebody praying for me ...

I've been spared by so many prayers ... How
many times I could not say ...
What a difference a prayer can make ... When
it's offered up in faith ...
God has always made a way ...When I didn't
know what to do ...
Just when I needed a miracle ... That's when
your prayers broke through ...
Somebody's praying for me ... Somebody's
knocking on Heaven's door ....
Somebody's praying for me ... Somebody's
lifting me up to the Lord ...

Well I knew it had to be ... Somebody down
on their knees ...
Somebody praying for me ...

Now I know that friend was you ...You were
the one God gave me ...
'Cuz when you prayed His love broke through.
It was your prayer that saved me
Thank you for praying for me ...Thank you for
knocking on Heaven's door ....
Thank you for praying for me ... Thank you for
lifting me up to the Lord ...
Now I can clearly see ...That you were the one
on your knees ...
So thank you for praying for me ...

Somebody's praying for me ... Somebody's
knocking on Heaven's door ....
Somebody's praying for me ... Somebody's
lifting me up to the Lord ...
Well I knew it had to be ... Somebody down
on their knees ...
Somebody praying for me ...

From the album "Uncharted Territory"
Don Moen and Claire Cloninger
(c)2011 Don Moen Music (ASCAP) / Juniper
Landing Music (ASCAP)
All rights reserved. Used by permission.

Chapter 14

Fall of the Gary

"Therefore, if anyone is in Christ, he is a new creation.
The old has passed away. Behold the new has come."
II Corinthians 5:17

*M*oving ahead patiently. Oxygen tank regulator turned higher for a greater flow. New call soon? Thanks to Dr. Vijay Misra, his four new stents unclogged jammed arteries. OK, so the heart's ready. Medical assistance notwithstanding, breathing issues worsen. The clinical trial bumped me for unhealthy side effects. Week long testing for inclusion on the wait list created new anxiety. What if I'm not eligible? Not in my hands and I have controlled what I could control. May 5, 2010 inclusion on transplant list (yippie moment) precipitated our move to Birmingham on May 23, 2010. First transplant opportunity on May 29, 2010 proved fruitless. So did calls #2, #3, #4 and call #5 on August 21st. Different reasons, but still no lung. Five trips, no transplant. Faith seemingly slipping a notch.

Through the devastating news Susan and I survived with love and prayers of family/friends. Oh, just for kicks, let's recall that back fracture. Talk about an "uh-oh" moment. Waiting for transplant, surviving diabetes with insulin, diet, and exercise, living with four stents around the heart, physical therapist Tina's frequent visits to our apartment aided physical preparation for transplantation. Tina pushed my envelope far beyond my expectations. With her smile, I didn't totally object. Well, maybe just a little. CaringBridge words share feelings from August 21st and 22nd.

SATURDAY, AUGUST 21, 2010 2:42 AM, CDT

"Wish we could tell you, a little before 3am, that Gary is in recovery after successful surgery ... until an hour ago, surgery was a possibility to start this weekend ... unfortunately, about 1:30 this morning we were informed that the lungs were not usable – the 5th trip of hope now turns into a waiting game for phone call #6 ... thanks for Rev. Charles Youngson of St. Thomas Episcopal in Birmingham who came and sat with us and prayed with us and anointed Gary and led us in prayer for the donor and tonight's potential recipients ... ironically, Mike Gibney came up to spend the day and was with us throughout the entire process tonight of getting a phone call (they are always unexpected), packing up for a 7–10 day hospital stay, driving to UAB, going through preliminary blood draw of 7 vials and then – the wait !! Then, news that tonight won't work ... Trust me

dear family and friends, your prayers and intercessions on our behalf are what keeps the Godwin boat afloat ... thanks for continuing to express your love for us in such a special way ... Susan and I love and appreciate all of you." Gary

SUNDAY, AUGUST 22, 2010 8:23 PM, CDT

"Gary and I are in the UAB hospital tonight, but not for a lung transplant. After resting and relaxing most of the day on Saturday (after the long night Friday waiting for possible lung), Gary took a spill at our apartment and we had to go to the ER around 8:30. He was in a great deal of pain and x-rays showed that he fractured his L3 on the spine. We spent eight hours in the ER, and he was then admitted into a hospital room at 5:30 this morning. He's in a back brace and on drugs to manage the pain. We hope he'll be discharged tomorrow, once we get it set up at home to make things safe so he can manage rehab and recovery. We were very disheartened last night (actually early morning) partially induced by so little sleep over two days, but have been encouraged today by visitors, phone calls, and scriptures. Thanks to Father Charles Youngson, who came this afternoon and shared prayers and Holy Communion with us ... it was a very special time, and to Parker (with wife Phyllis, part of our Birmingham family) who came over just to hang out. Please pray for rapid healing and recovery for Gary, and sleep and rest for me. Once again we are extremely blessed by wonderful medical care, compassionate and caring nurses, and the angels of UAB. We love you and we are so humbled & honored to walk with such amazing friends & family." Susan

Phone conversation with my mom usually produces calm, loving words amplifying her recent activities, including her latest doctor visit. Speaking across the 343-mile separation between Birmingham and New Orleans, my throat "tickle" stopped being funny. Snoffs (Susan's combination word for simultaneous sneeze and cough) turned my talk into juvenile gibberish. Reacting with speed and intention, I thrust my cellular toward Susan's outstretched hand. Quickly needing cough medicine from the bathroom I rose from my chair in a flash, simultaneously taking a left hand turn. My Alabama two-step didn't replicate a dance. Dizziness rapidly overcame steadiness as I began my corkscrew descent to the floor. One problem. Our bedroom door jamb slowed the fall. The expense was high. Fractured L3 vertebrae. "Susan, get our neighbor, but first a freezer ice pack for my back" I plaintively uttered. Grasping freshly vacuumed carpet, with a mouth tasting threads of the carpet weave, crawling to bed and rising from the floor expended any remnant of energy. It hurt too. The extended hand of Jesus helped my three foot pull from floor to bed. Numbing effect of the freezer pack brought blessed relief.

Thanks to good neighbor Rob for contacting Rocky Ridge Fire and Rescue only a few hundred yards removed from our accommodations. Backboard and gurney transported me from apartment to ambulance with ice pack the only comfort during the siren wailing ride to UAB. Wait. I'm at UAB for a *lung*. ER treatment included pain killers and confirming x-ray about the L3 fracture. I'm convinced our lives include three residences: primary home in Fairhope, temporary apartment in Birmingham, and UAB. Back brace, pain medications and a private room serve the required purpose during this unscheduled visit. "But I'm here for a lung." Six day journal entry trail lost in a paper shuffle that accompanied two back and forth trips to UAB within a week. Regardless of this latest temporary diversion I'm still thinking about that lung.

Hello Tina. Welcome back. Not lungs but this time a back issue. Complimenting her smile, I wrongly believed, would produce a lightened workload. Haha. Her therapy notebook brought new chapters devoted to back patients. Toughest for me was the "log roll" getting into and out of bed. With no position comfortable, a slow roll was my next best option. Increased need for bathroom visits (any movement seemed excruciating) necessitated an alternative. "Susan, where is that urinal?" Welcome major relief from minimized motion. Tina's exercise regimen started slowly (remember we crawl, then walk, then run). Following visits increased my pace. The love-hate relationship which develops between patient and therapist became full blown. Loving Tina for what she made me do, I gave equal time to not loving Tina for what she made me do. Push, push, push. If she hadn't pushed, I'd probably still be in the crawling phase of recovery. Thanks Tina.

Reflection: Another memory bank withdrawal. I am reminded of youthful years when riding a merry-go-round was a fun excursion. Recalling the whistle like musical pipes in the background hastened return to an earlier, calmer life style. Today's see-saw circular ride seems to accomplish nothing. Time to stop the music. Slip the stirrups of my plastic painted horse. Stop the up and down, round-and-round motion still going nowhere. In God's time. Checking the 20-20 rearview mirror, it's apparent these earlier trials served as preparation for my new lung and new life. How much does God put on your plate? How do you respond? Angry, frustrated, disappointed, disillusioned? How many times does He put a roadblock in your path? How often do you praise Him with your words and disappoint Him with your deeds? Willful children ask "are you still walking alongside me, Lord? How much more can we take? Dare I even ask?" Do you know when it's time to surrender? Finally, not knowing the outcome but putting faith in His hands, shortly before the sixth and final call I said, "Lord, I'm yours. Amen." He knew it all along.

Tina and pre-exercise happiness

CHAPTER 15

HERE COME THE LUNG . . .
HERE COME THE LUNG

⤝

"Rejoice always, pray without ceasing,
give thanks in all circumstances..."
I Thessalonians 5:16 - 18

*L*ost. Gone. Forever history. Which part of today becomes memorable history and which part swiftly disappears? Following surgery, days truly lost tumble from the mind's memory. Physician visitation prior to surgery included information about possible post surgical "issues." Minor problems became expectations. Looming unexpected however was the large surprise awaiting in the SICU recovery suite.

7:20am CDT Tuesday, September 28, 2010. *Again. Same message. Ho-hum. "Mr. Godwin, this is UAB transplant. We may have a lung for you." Really. Familiar sounds and sentences (wish I'd consumed those grits earlier). The routine previously unknown now part of transplant history. Updated info transmitted to family. "Sorry to disturb you. I got another call from UAB. Probably nothing, but we'll let you know. By the way, I'm the 'backup.' Primary recipient needs both lungs and initial indications are two good lungs. But, we're prepared." I never suspected the surprise following transplant.*

Day 128 in my journal, Tuesday, September 28, 2010:

"7:20am—"You are the backup recipient. Nothing to eat or drink and get to the 5th floor as soon as you can.' So for the 6th time clean up, pack up and head to UAB. First time to deal with morning traffic. Rev. Charles Youngson came to visit and offered prayer. Dr. Octavio Pajaro (transplant surgeon) came by. I'm backup to a double lung, and if transplanted I'll get a left lung. Dr. Pajaro said we should know something in a couple of hours. Patience. Wait. Again."

OK Michael, potential primary recipient, get ready. Arriving from south Mississippi Michael soon discovers the process is no quick "in and out" procedure. Donate some blood. Check vital signs. Puff up the chest for x-rays. "Deep breath . . . hold it . . . breathe." Sign paperwork. Though the routine was familiar Susan and I detected distinct differences. Immediately, no donation requested for the Godwin blood bank. No quick x-ray pix of the lungs. No IV in preparation for surgery. No EKG hookup. No vitals (blood pressure, pulse, temperature, weight). No offer given to hook into the UAB oxygen supply (though I did receive this service upon request). HTICU recliner chair the only familiar connection to five prior visits. Having missed breakfast, Susan and I began conversation about favored places to eat. Arrival of primary recipient Michael dashed hopes for our transplant today. Settling in his recliner, relaxation followed a long drive from south Mississippi. Susan and I snickered as breakfast possibilities (McDonald's serves until 10:30 am, right?) turned into brunch opportunities. "Does Chappy's serve brunch or just lunch?" A diabetic needs to maintain a fairly regular eating regimen. With time ticking away, and a pleading, empty stomach, I felt the "woozies" that follow no food intake. Few life events match the cantankerous nature of an empty stomach. Hunger pangs filtered from stomach to brain. As a potential surgical patient, I knew food and beverages were no-no's. However, a diabetic condition needs exception status and Susan agreed. A cracker or two might have passed security; never tasted better.

Moving past the brunch hour Susan and I, both feeling a bit humored by our recollection of restaurants visited during our stay, began discussing late lunches. "How about Newk's? They're nearby." "Unless you want some meat and we go to Arby's." "The Fish Market (a favorite lunch spot of ours) only two blocks away." Food diverted our attention from the tension of waiting. We played our new game, "name that restaurant," recalling most of the eating establishments frequented during our stay. Smiles and laughter broke the solemn silence of Michael and the medical staff present when we recalled our hibachi experience.

With son Matthew in town, and following Sunday church services, we opted for a Japanese restaurant. Coming before transplant, my tethered oxygen container nestled alongside our seats around the hibachi grill. Laughter at the chef's food prep show quickly turned to horror. Reality flared as we realized the huge fireball created for his act was within arm's length of the oxygen stuffing my nasal passages. Oxygen and fire. Not an appealing combination. "Rightee tightee, leftee loosee" quickly flowed from the brain as I fumbled with the oxygen regulator, seeking the "tightee" position. Got it. More humor. More laughter. Michael nearby still sitting in silent anticipation.

Past the lunch hour, Susan and I discussed early dinner possibilities. No hibachi, but everything else was on the table. Hey, maybe a buffet? The place to eat became less important than food to eat but our humor never waned. Remembering God's time, we were convinced no transplant today. Oops.

Joy sometimes accompanies progress of the process. Sometimes there is sadness. Michael needed two lungs. The donor could offer but one. Words I had awaited since May 5, 2010 transplant listing: "We're going to transplant Mr. Godwin." Activity blossoms like Mobile's azaleas in the springtime. A certain numbness paralyzes my entire body upon hearing the news. All the pieces of the process connect as transformation begins for this well defined, giant jigsaw puzzle.

3:30pm — and here we go! Sorry Michael (primary recipient declined because only one lung was usable and he needed both). Not your turn. Been there before. It's a pain and I'm sad for you. And Matthew's on his way. And in the prep room we wait, and wait, and wait with patience. Thank you God. Amen."

Two thoughts: #1. Finally, I turned the waiting over to God. The first four times I felt in charge (remember call #4?). Nothing happened. Call #5? Same result. This time I let God take care of matters, and it led to lung transplant. Thought #2. The humorous stories mentioned reflect our desire, almost obsession, for food. Where to eat breakfast? Brunch? Lunch? Dinner? Transplant prep made meals a moot point. Who needs food?

Familiar routine takes place. There's the Godwin blood bank donation. Here come the IV's. Hook up to the EKG machine. Why don't they warm those leads before attachment to your body? Heart rate good. Body temp OK. EKG indicates heart beat. Oxygen level acceptable. Shaving from shoulder to thigh. All familiar and probably sad for Michael to watch. Belongings packed, his southbound path led home to await his call #2. Food thoughts disappeared. "Is it really happening this time?" Outward appearances became reality as the gurney journey proceeded to the surgical suite.

6:55pm. Palm cross couldn't make my trip but safely tucked in Susan's hands prior to our pre-surgical kiss goodbye. The word "goodbye" evoked a different sensation this time. Professionally efficient, the surgical staff mood seemed compatible with the room temperature. Reminder to self: these folks are on a mission they have decided to accept and I am that mission. Case closed. Brilliantly lighted and more than adequately staffed, the cold surgical suite and bed became my new support for the next few hours. Prior to anes-thesia induced sleep, remembering that the mission is subject to being "scrubbed" up until the first incision, my mind becomes a whirlwind of questions. Too late. Goodnight Gary. Recalling my final thought prior to "nite-nite," I looked above the surgical mask into the anesthesiologist's eyes and that thought dissipated as drugs controlled. My own shuttered eyes rendered the question forgotten and sleep consumed my body until the next day. So much for one who loves to be in control.

Following a successful two-hour, forty-five minute procedure, and into the next day, my new life rose concurrently with Birmingham's Wednesday morning sun. Recovery mode, viewing the horizon on this September 29, 2010, nothing could prepare me for a day in my life "lost" somewhere. My memory bank erased. All deposits withdrawn. Nothing. Zilch. Nada. Zero. My 14-hour "nap" led to a void in my life's memory bank. Though chatty as a prisoner locked in solitary for a month, my frantic search reveals no recollection of any conversation. Nothing revealed. Blame the drugs. Since surgery drugs have become a well worn excuse. Though non-existent in my mind chatter was incredibly vivid in the hearts of my visitors: Susan, Matthew, Victor, Louise, Phyllis, Parker and Charles Youngson. But, I had a new lung. A lost day proved to be the least of my concerns.

Just as the 29th became a blank chip in my computer brain, the 30th held new sensations, not totally unexpected but for the severity of a perceived complication. Can you say heart attack? Two new stents to join the four on the other side of my heart. Seeking answers from the medical personnel assembled, I questioned: "I'm having a little bit of pain between my nipples; is that usual for post surgery?" A trip to the O.R. answered that question. No doubt about the pain just no sense of what it was. I discovered later that blood pressure readings and heart rate were both abnormal, and I was to head immediately to the O.R. Two more stents. Two days added to an already modest number of days of hospitalization. Too much to fathom. Too much to be thankful for. Too big a miracle. A feeling that carried me through most of our 188-day stay in Birmingham. And once again Lord I commend my life and my life's work to You, with thanks for a family still newly grieving over loss of my donor's life. He promises to never give us more than we can handle, "... but I feel pretty close Lord!"

Reflection: Major surgery entails physical changes to a body. No argument here. Following surgery, complications are not unexpected. However, major medical issues (heart attack) are quite a stunner for someone two days post transplant. Patients are told to expect difficulties, answering the question "Why stay in the hospital and the Birmingham area for six to eight weeks after transplant?" Best place to be when problems arise, that's why. Time before, during and after critical surgery seems to pass painfully slow. Resist the temptation to be a time piece watcher. This time in the transplant process reminds me of a spiritual weekend which included the surrender of watches, clocks, or any form of time piece. Staff understands the schedule and nothing is done on other than God's time. His time rules. Period. For me, six reminder visits to UAB all confirm God's time. When do you usually arrive for appointments? Early? On time? Late? If you feel in control, everyone operates on your time; or so you think. What time factor do you remember exactly? Birth of a child or grandchild? Time of your wedding (don't forget the anniversary)? When to "spring forward" and when to "fall back?" Time. The wonderful wound healer. Put yourself in His hands and remember all things happen in His time. Do we understand the word eternity? Endless.

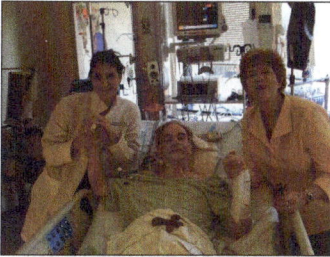

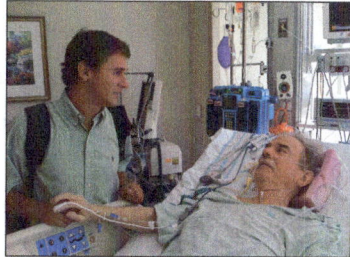

Dr. Hecker, Susan and Matthew on the 1st day
following transplant
One day before heart attack

CHAPTER 16

STEPS

"...the righteousness of God is revealed from faith for faith, as it is written, the righteous shall live by faith."
Romans 1:17

*F*ootsteps. Stair steps. Dance steps. Side steps. Baby steps. Crawling begins our lifetime progression of ambulation. Steps. Movement. Gleeful bursts of laughter from parent and baby introduce the era of walking. Happy giggles and shrieks herald the first rapid steps that turn into running. Steps. Taken for granted, we gain greater appreciation for steps when first we stumble and fall. Ouch! "Maybe this step thing isn't so great after all," we mumble while slowly rising to our feet, checking for bruises and abrasions. Rapid erasure of the memory terminates the fear associated with walking and running and with renewed faith we return to our love of steps.

Ambulation. How many steps comprise a lifetime of being on our feet? Grocery shopping? Exercising? Weekend shopping? Climbing steps to an elevated store or restaurant? Holiday shopping? Steps all day clerking in a store? Walking up a flight of stairs at home or work? Steps become an under appreciated aspect of daily living when legs and feet move in rhythm to our desires. Broken bones in the leg, sprains in the upper or lower ankle, blisters from new shoes all diminish our ability to take "normal" steps. Ever walk assisted by a cane, crutches, or walker? Ride in a wheelchair because of leg injury, disease, or physical weakness? Seek transport support to move from point A to point B? Before IPF, walking anywhere provided an enjoyable experience. After IPF diagnosis? Increasing shortness of breath accompanied me step for step. Leaving the apartment complex at least one canister of oxygen always accompanied our travels.

October 13, 2009. Remember the date. My journey ventured north from Fairhope to Birmingham and a first visit with UAB's pulmonary transplant team. Short steps and my portable oxygen supply sustained me from Kirklin Clinic's front door to the bank of elevators transporting physically impaired patients. Susan's travels to Kirklin's 5th floor found her favorite patient awaiting appointment with a pulmonary doc. Quick scan reveals similarity between the pulmonary patient waiting area and an oxygen supply showroom. Patient transport (helpful employees moving patients confined to wheelchairs) seems to maintain a never ending presence. Wheeling in; wheeling out. Thinking how sad to need this transport, my view changed with my first ride. Good health Gary in a wheelchair. A fairly huge humility check. IPF takes a lot out of its victims. A lot.

The visit with Dr. Victor Thannickal offered early indication that IPF would cut short the number of steps left in my lifetime. OK, so my steps are limited. Faithfully, just one more reason for joyful anticipation of the day when lung transplant occurs. Once again time to step out and following transplant my donor steps out with me.

Bit of a "side-step" first. Susan and I opened arms to Tina the physical therapist who crossed our paths shortly after my fall and L3 fracture on August 22nd. The warmth of her smile eased the pain associated with rehabilitation exercises. Baby steps at first. Hardly any steps at all, but that's part of the recovery. Ten minute walks in our apartment breezeway indicated success for a "major" goal; six hundred seconds of baby steps. Though I could step freely on my own assistance was nearby if needed. On later visits Tina moved our steps from the breezeway to the parking lot. Still not ready for a marathon I'm stepping out in faith with God's angel Tina. In an ironic twist of fate, the night before my final scheduled therapy session with Tina became the night of my transplant. Not to worry though. Tina now returns for a new round of therapy, including "steps," following my return from transplant. Once again it's time to crawl before walking and running.

Humorous side note. One of my first ventures "out" following transplant was to share a special meal with Susan, Matthew and our scientist friend Dr. Louise Hecker at a noted

Birmingham restaurant. Needing momentary relief I inquired of a server the location of the men's room. Directing my path, while pointing to his right, he politely said, "Through those doors, up the stairs, it's on the right." "Up the stairs?" "Why not put the *ladies'* room upstairs?" I questioned to no one in particular. Steps. Fresh from surgery, still a bit uneasy on my feet, and I've got to climb steps. There was an option but I didn't bring an extra pair of pants. "OK buddy what's it going to be?" Standing at the foot of the seven steps leading to a platformed resting area, I prayed: "Lord, one step at a time. Please help. It is now that I need you to carry me!"

God heard and responded. Up seven, no problem. Feeling good, but not cocky, seven steps remained. Negotiated them, quietly expelled a y-e-e-s-s-s, gave a small fist pump and looked forward to the trip down. I almost forgot my reason for climbing those steps. Smiling broadly upon return to the dinner table I shared the story with my dining companions. Smiles all around. Ironically, the date was October 13th, my one year anniversary from the first visit to UAB on this transplant journey. Joyfully on this same day I relinquished to transplant coordinator Lanier the fifty-seven staples which had closed my incision. God's time or coincidence? My journal's final words for this day? "*. . . and I climbed fourteen stairs.* THANKS LORD." Gary and GiGi (newly named left lung)

Reflection. Today is October 8, 2010. Return to the apartment just eleven days after hospital admittance. Incredibly joyful day but sad for leaving the professional caregivers who helped restore my life to normal living. Shedding tears along the way, Susan and I walked gingerly to the bank of elevators for the trip to the 2nd floor parking garage. As a main thoroughfare, the walkway from Kirklin Clinic to the parking garage witnesses all makes and models: doctors, nurses, UAB employees, patients, families, friends, young, not-so-young — a microcosm of life. And I was walking out after eleven incredible days, without supplemental oxygen or any assistance for my steps. No wheelchair. No walker. No cane or crutches. No support (though Susan was next to me). What steps in life are you not taking? What steps can you take as a leap of faith? Who offers support for your steps when needed?

When it comes to steps the first is always the hardest.

P.S. to Reflection: The sensation of my first steps with a new lung? Saddened at the termination of a life that continues to live in me and blessed for my new life. Midway through those approximately 45 or so steps in the covered walkway, heading to the parking garage, I paused long enough to view a varied collection of humanity passing nearby. Oxygen supporting some, wheelchairs transporting some and ID-carded employees on a fast pace to their appointed rounds. Leaning against the window frame, collecting my thoughts, Susan asked if I was okay. "I need just a few moments," uttered the words from a crackling voice with tears brushing my cheeks as angel wings. Steps.

Post transplant with Dr. Thannickal

CHAPTER 17

SIGNS OF NEW LIFE

*"I waited patiently for the Lord; he inclined
to me and heard my cry"
Psalm 40:1*

Stepping into recovery. Riding the rails of a new adventure. Treasured moments abound. Old friends and new alongside for the entire trip. Easy to feel a forceful wind when your sails have been trimmed and refitted. Body almost new, yet stout enough to chase that UAB lung transplant record: somewhere in the 20+ year post surgery neighborhood. Thanks along the way for special folks not seen often enough: nieces Jennifer and Melissa, brother Wayne, sister Sue, Vera, Sal, Taylor, Bill, Reggie, Daria, Midge, Jean, Rusty, Mady, Mary Hair, Jim, Diana, Lee, Linda, Marcia, "lunch bunch" and communications director Bruce. Follow these signs of new life and reflections from the journey:

#1. Birmingham's Railroad Park. Reclamation project for a former eyesore along the downtown railroad tracks. Susan, her sister Betsy and I enjoyed an outdoor musicfest during opening weekend. After surgery, Matthew, Susan and I walk without my oxygen container up an incline for the first time since transplant. A wow moment that intrigues me: Railroad Park, former ugly downtown sight, transformed into a beautiful reflection of renewal. My new lung? A personal reclamation project. Sign of new life.

#2. The UAB bell-ringing tradition indicates successful surgery and care for a transplant patient soon to vacate his 5th floor HTICU accommodations. Whispered conversation overheard indicated my lung may have transplanted from a young person. I questioned a doctor, "would that make me young?" "Gary, you might have a young lung," came the reply, "but still a 67-year old body." One final bit of medical humor. HTICU. Checked in 9.28.10 and checked out 10.8.10. Changes? Heart attack, two new stents, lung transplant all within 11 days, and I walk away. Tearfully leaving caregivers I ring the bell, gratefully tolling for Susan and me. Thoughts for those assembled: Give me the hug, give me the tear. I ring the bell, disappear. Sign of new life.

#3. Parker and Phyllis. Along with UAB and a staff of caregivers, our most prized new friendship. Strangers turned friends who opened their home and hearts. Gracious hospitality always abounds at the P&P B&B. Susan and I reserve the "Godwin Suite" for regular UAB follow-ups. Parker's culinary offerings worthy of inclusion on an Emeril menu.

Phyllis' retirement years offering a "tithe plus" of hours available in a day for church activities, when not following athletic achievements of grandchildren. Their remodeled home and my left lung, both signs of new life.

#4. Surprise gift. Perpetual pleading provides a weekend pass for travels home (for the first time in six months) to attend a special "family" wedding. Ryan and Kasey. Newest daughter-in-law for spiritual brother Mike and sister-in-law for Kelley and Jason. Feels like bindings unbound for this early release program. Oops, not released yet. One final week of up close and personal care. Freedom's coming and a sign of new life.

#5. Keeping the promise for a special friend — Tomba. Italian greyhound loved and nurtured by Dr. Louise Hecker. Such a part of the research office space his collar included a personal ID card. How did he swipe it? I committed to Dr. Hecker, and Tomba, a post transplant personal romp when I could walk six blocks from Tomba's home to a favorite dog park. His svelte powerful body strained my right arm as we maneuvered up the street, down to the park, up the steps again and down to home. Mission complete. Thanks Tomba. Sadly, health issues leading to seizures brought rapid demise. Dr. Hecker agonizing over a life terminating decision. While Louise slept, Tomba trotted the path to doggy heaven. One final, loving expression; the decision no longer belonging to Louise. "I don't cry because you're gone. I smile because I had time to know you." Now romping with friends in doggy heaven, for Tomba, sign of new life.

Reflection: One in one hundred. Statistical odds of lung transplant for those in need. More blessed by this miracle than I could ever imagine, I grieve for the ninety-nine. I grieve for my donor's family and those losing loved ones. I grieve that organ donation remains less prevalent than needs to be filled. I grieve for departed friends. Mo. John. Jim. The other Charles Gary. Brian. Mickey. I grieve for those living with new circumstances. I marvel at my miracle. Maybe you can help provide for others. Organ donor? Thanks. Consider the possibilities if you aren't. For somebody, somewhere, sometime a donor organ will be a sign of new life.

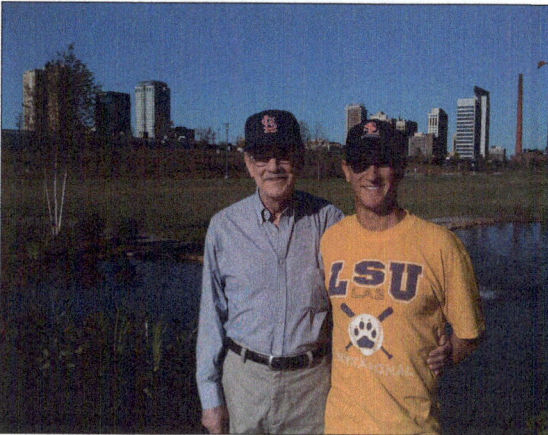

Matthew joining first post surgery outing at Birmingham's downtown reclamation project

Dr. Hecker and Tomba after doggy park romp
fulfilling my post transplant commitment

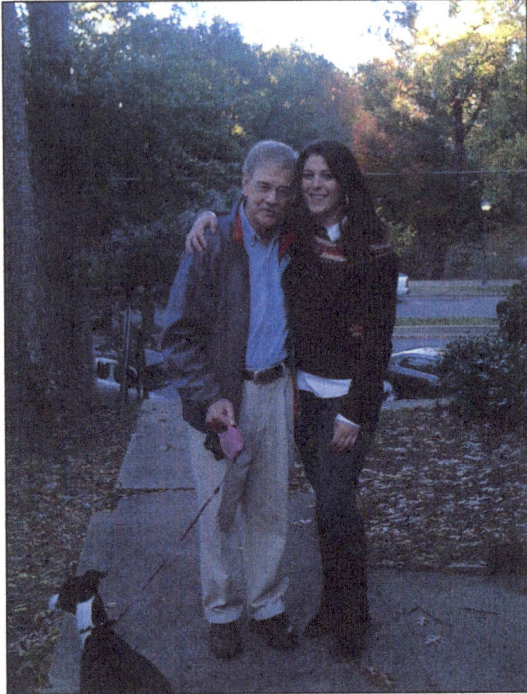

RESOURCE CORNER

Alabama Organ Center
Suite 102
500 22nd Street South
Birmingham, AL
(P) 1.800.252.3677
(F) 205.731.9250 email: alabamaorgancenter.org

UAB Transplant
1107 Jefferson Tower
625 19th Street South
Birmingham, AL 35294
(P) 205.975.8615
(F) 205.975.9792 email: uabmedicine.org (choose letter T)

UNOS
United Network for Organ Sharing
P. O. Box 2484
Richmond, VA 23218
(P) 888.894.6361 email: unos.org

Pulmonary Fibrosis Foundation
811 West Evergreen Avenue, Suite 204
Chicago, Illinois 60642-2642
(P) 888.733.6741
(F) 866.587.9158 email: pulmonaryfibrosis.org

ByRonPalmCross®

(P) 309-787-5640

(F) 309-787-7050 email: palmcrossesbyron.com

CaringBridge.org

1715 Yankee Doodle Road

Suite 301

Eagan, MN 55121

(P) 651.452.7940

(F) 651.681.7115 email:caringbridge.org

CHAPTER 18

BELIEVING IN ANGELS

⚜

"Do not neglect to show hospitality to strangers, for thereby some have entertained angels unawares."
Hebrews 13:2

Trepidation. Uncertainty. Fright. Nope. Not transplant intimidation. All three signify my approach to this chapter. Possible memory failure might lead to exclusion of God's angels in this segment of heart notes. Fear not. If you remember me, I remember you. Maybe not by name, but certainly by the joyful love you exhibited during our Birmingham stay of 188 days. Too many protective, caring moments illuminate lives which reflect the presence of angels. Your life probably recalls a moment or two when angel wings fluttered on your behalf. Names and circumstances might be different but you knew when angelic action touched your life. Maybe some actions shown happened to you during a time of crisis and need. With fear of missing specifically named angels, here are a few memorable moments with family and friends:

Brother Wayne and son Matthew. Yard landscaping and needed household repairs during Fairhope visits starting from Charlotte NC and Mobile. Thanks for Matthew's immediate visit post surgery and Wayne and his wife Vera's visit to celebrate my birthday. Family. Thanks also to sister Sue, unable to join us physically because of primary responsibilities as New Orleans connection for our 94 year old mother. Thanks Sue for developing and maintaining and linking an incredibly lengthy prayer chain.

Julie and daughter Corte, our first official Birmingham visitors. Friends bringing items missed during packing. Two beautiful angels bringing a slice of "home heaven." Surgical recovery assisted with gracious use of "Bear-ster Lodge."

David & Georgi. Our last official visitors. Georgi's hand crocheted scarf gifted by David. A warm reminder that Birmingham's winter chill capabilities included attacks on an exposed and susceptible neck and throat. David's best gift? The journal for keeping notes about our Birmingham stay. Never much of a writer, potential early mortality provided impetus for more intentionality in daily journal entries.

Tonja and Mae. Care coordinators for clinical trials. Procured oxygen when there was a foulup in Birmingham with new oxygen supplier. Oxygen angels.

Shelia. Michael. Daisy. Larry. Gary. Brian. Gail. Mickey. Sterling. Unknown strangers becoming friends through common problem of IPF. Joint ministry.

Ceil. Another church friend bringing a slice of home on her way through town, sharing a dinner celebrating our ninth wedding anniversary.

Mike. Hometown spiritual brother. Walked through the transplant process during his visit when I received call #5. Still owe him a yogurt.

Fr. Robert Seawell. Fr. Mark DiCristina. Priests from home church close by Mobile Bay in southern Alabama. Multiple visits during our stay, surgery, post surgery and heart attack. Special Communion service with Fr. Mark and Christian singer-songwriter Lynn DeShazo.

Christian Copyright Solutions (CCS) staff. Kept God's business afloat – and growing – during our six month absence.

Rev. Charles Youngson. Priest at St. Thomas Episcopal who became "our" man of God during time in Birmingham. Thanks also to Karen and Glandion from St. Peter's Anglican for visits and ministry during difficult transition in their parish.

The Stroom connection. Eric, Julie, Parker, Phyllis, Erica and Brian. Room at Erica and Brian's plus Erica's culinary delight betraying her self described infancy in the kitchen. Parker and Phyllis graciously offering Vestavia Hills accommodations. Frequent visits turned a private bathroom and bedroom into the affectionately named "Godwin Suite." What a B&B from P&P. The glue binding this family? Eric and Julie the loving relationship connectors providing the spark to ignite these friendships.

Debbie and Stanley. Incredibly amazing dynamite duo. Neighbors who watched over the small piece of His creation entrusted to our care. Kept up with authorized guests in our home. Neighbors like Debbie and Stanley are a wonderful gift and great friends exhibiting true Christian spirit.

Tony and Chris, whose own grounds are worthy of consideration for "yard of the month" twelve times a year. Green thumbs kept bushes professionally trimmed and garden beds weeded (yuck job). Sports buddies and tender hearts for absent friends.

Church of the Apostles (COTA) family. Weekly updates on my progress shared by Fr. Robert and Fr. Mark. Cheryl's administrative notes kept us in touch with the church and friends in need and her visit was a welcome relief for Susan. Blessings also for long time friends at St. Luke's Church and St. Luke's School. Wonderful memories.

Frank and Suzanne. Hot dogs. Ice cream bars. Peach cobbler. Loving friends with whom we share occasional "hot dog night." Helped with home landscaping chores before our move to Birmingham. Multiple visits to include post stent insertion in April, "relief visit" for Susan to have time on her own away from caregiving role (Suzanne is a nurse) and Susan's birthday weekend celebration. Frank, my dear friend with extensive talents and intense desire to share those talents with his less knowledgeable buddy. A good friend with a kindly ear. What a better world if filled with Franks and Suzannes.

My soul mate. My gentle spirit. My comforter and guide. My fellow traveler on a life journey never imagined. My friend.

My love. My wife. This ongoing journey does not exist without my sweet Susan.

No problem thanking Susan or any others mentioned. However, I shared my apprehensive dilemma with a dear friend. "I'm sure I will miss someone." "Gary, you need a bigger book for all the loving folks you met these past months." Unforgettable final words from that friend? "You may not cite them by name, or personally thank them, but they know your heart will always be thankful." Charles Gary Godwin

Christmas 2011

Chapter 19

Day 188 - Good Bye Birmingham

"I heard the voice of the Lord saying,
'Whom shall I send and who shall go for us?'
Then I said, 'Here am I. Send me.' "
Isaiah 6:8

Day 188 - 11.27.10 – Bye, Bye Birmingham. Thank you!!

" The day we leave to return to Fairhope happens to be the last page of this journal. Don't tell me this isn't one more miraculous God thing — Thank you, thank you, thank you!! Lord, you have led us through quite an experience and have never left our side. Thanks for sending (nephew) Sean to help (pack and move). Thanks for good neighbor Rob. Thanks for all the angels you sent to us. And now, it's on with our lives and the work you give us to do. Help us accomplish what you desire. As we close the

chapter of our Birmingham stay, lead us to your next task. We leave at 1:15 pm this day. Two days after Thanksgiving, Saturday November 27, 2010, 5:27pm, CST, we end our trip. WELCOME HOME! Thanks Lord for the miraculous ride. Amen." Charles Gary Godwin

Give the hug; shed the tear; ring the bell; disappear . . ...

November 27, 2010. No tethered oxygen.

No mechanical assistance.

Susan and I close the door one last time on apartment #822.

One-half year ago the adventure began.

188 days later we return home to family and friends

left behind.

New lung. New man. New life.

Thank you Lord.

POST SCRIPT

I llness debilitates. Sickness swiftly saps strength. Patient and caregiver equally taxed. Recovery usually takes longer than anticipated. Slow, cautious movement returning to your pre-illness form serves as the preferred, judicious course. Impaired judgment prevails, though, and sensible solutions soar as if on eagle wings.

Adults face a different challenge with children. Parents learn early that illness is a part of childhood. We grow up somewhat oblivious to the harshness of illness and injury suffered as part of our aging years. Playing much beyond our athletic years usually requires proximity from the playing field to the hospital. Diminishing reflexes, dimming eyesight, an inflating ring-around-the-middle, sore/aching knees, legs, arms and joints racing rapidly toward arthritis signify the road to physical retirement lies shortly ahead. Could that be a reasonable explanation for an aging population driven to less strenuous sporting activities?

Aches and pains associated with physical activities tend to prevail sooner in our advancing years. Our search expands for more sedate methods of keeping an active life style. We make the choices. Visits to our physicians come more rapidly. Despite all our best efforts, we find ourselves smack dab in the cross hairs of the mortality rifle as it aims to gun us down. Death offers no escape. Armed with that knowledge, we fight to extend the sand in our hourglass.

Certain illnesses typically engulf most of the population. Generally, a small dose of medication reverses adverse impacts on the body. Some circumstances mandate more intentional treatment. Thankfully, the human body provides parts which can be interchangeable. Organ donation and transplantation offer new hope for lives whose mortality seemed imminent. Dawning of each new day reminds me of the miracle offered by a donor I may never know. As a living poster child for organ donation, transplant surgery and continuing research I urge you to consider becoming an organ donor. Certain instances involve being a living donor. My sister-in-law donated a kidney to her husband and both now live fulfilling lives.

Thanks for your support of this book. Proceeds will help fund research efforts for IPF and education about organ dona-tion. As you reach crossroads in your life may your faith sus-tain you and remember who walks alongside on your life's journey. His peace rests with you and, if needed, transplant faith! Amen.

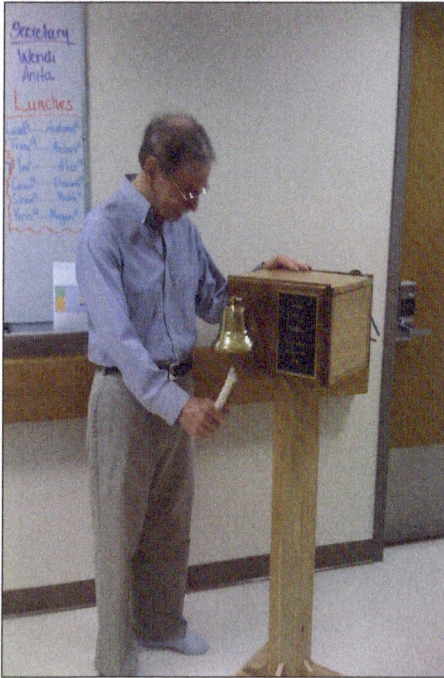

"The Bell"

CPSIA information can be obtained at www.ICGtesting.com
Printed in the USA
LVOW010712090413

328271LV00002B/2/P